MADONNA

MADONNA

The unofficial and unauthorised biography of
MADONNA
by Victoria Chow

Published by
Kandour Ltd
1-3 Colebrook Place
London N1 8HZ

This edition printed in 2004 for
Bookmart Limited
Registered Number 2372865
Trading as Bookmart Ltd
Blaby Road
Wigston
Leicester LE18 4SE

First published June 2004

ISBN 1–904756–12–3

Production services:
Metro Media Ltd

Author: Victoria Chow

With thanks to: Jenny Ross, Emma Hayley,
Lee Coventry, Belinda Weber, Nick Bradshaw

Cover design: Mike Lomax
Cover Image: Rex Features

Inside Images: Rex Features

© Kandour Ltd

Printed and bound by Nørhaven Paperback, Denmark

MADONNA

FOREWORD

This series of biographies is a celebration of celebrity. It features some of the world's greatest modern-day icons including movie stars, soap personalities, pop idols, comedians and sporting heroes. Each biography examines their struggles, their family background, their rise to stardom and in some cases their struggle to stay there. The books aim to shed some light on what makes a star. Why do some people succeed when others fail?

Written in a light-hearted and lively way, and coupled with the most up-to-date details on the world's favourite heroes and heroines, this series is an entertaining read for anyone interested in the world of celebrity. Discover all about their career highlights – what was the defining moment to propel them into superstardom? No story about fame is without its ups and downs. We reveal the emotional rollercoaster ride that many of these stars have been on to stay at the top. Read all about your most adored personalities in these riveting books.

MADONNA

CONTENTS

MADONNA

Full name:
Madonna Louise Veronica Ciccone Ritchie
Eye colour: Hazel
Date of birth: 16 August 1958
Place of birth: Bay City, Michigan, USA
Height: 5'4 1/2"
Present partner: Guy Ritchie (husband)
Daughter: Lourdes Maria Ciccone Leon (Lola), born 14 April 1996; father Carlos Leon
Son: Rocco John Ritchie, born 11 August 2000; father Guy Ritchie
Marriages:
Sean Penn (16 August 1985–10 January 1989); Guy Ritchie (22 December 2000–present day)

Star sign: Leo
The monarchs of the zodiac, Leos are generous, broadminded and dramatic, although a Leo can also be a bit of a bully. Leos think that they are always right – and they usually are!

MADONNA

Chinese birth sign: Dog
Loyal, forthright and honest, Dogs are protective of those they love. They have quick tempers, and are leaders who don't take it well when others try and tell them what to do.

Career highlight to date:
Evita (1996): Finally merging her acting and singing talents, Madonna proved her critics wrong when she won the Golden Globe for Best Performance by an Actress in a Motion Picture – Comedy/Musical. Her recording of *Don't Cry For Me Argentina* and the soundtrack album also proved to be big sellers.

MADONNA

Bruce Willis auditioned for the role of Madonna's boyfriend in the 1985 film *Desperately Seeking Susan*. The part eventually went to Robert Joy. Willis went on to appear in the television series *Moonlighting* that same year. He has since starred in movies such as *Die Hard* and *Pulp Fiction*.

Madonna's popular hit *Vogue* was taken from the album that accompanied Madonna's 1990 movie *Dick Tracy*. Called *I'm Breathless* — a reference to her character in the film, Breathless Mahoney.

Introduction

MADONNA

INTRODUCTION

ack in 1984 MTV launched its Video Music Awards. The inaugural ceremony featured one of the nominees for the Best New Artist Award performing her soon-to-be-released single *Like a Virgin* on a stage dominated by a gigantic white wedding cake. That artist was Madonna. The 26-year-old singer was dressed in a white bridal outfit consisting of a bustier, skirt and veil, accessorised with her trademark Boy Toy belt and numerous strands of pearls and crucifixes. She writhed around on the stage and simulated sex in front of the audience, no one was going to forget this performance – or indeed the artist – in a hurry.

MADONNA

INTRODUCTION

For the 20th Video Music Awards ceremony in 2003 it was decided that two of the pop world's leading talents Britney Spears and Christina Aguilera would sing a tribute to Madonna, who was considered the Queen of Pop.

Everyone thought they had Madonna figured out in early 2003. The former Material Girl had become Maternal Girl, giving up causing controversy to look after her two children and set up home in England with husband Guy Ritchie. The former wild child had settled down and become respectable. The new Madonna would not do anything to shock the establishment anymore... would she?

The MTV audience went wild when Spears and Aguilera burst on to the stage dressed in Madonna's 1984 bridal style, complete with lace gloves, garters and layers of jewellery. The two sang *Like a Virgin* and completed their duet with similarly suggestive gyrations that the Material Girl had shocked the industry with 19 years before.

Then the music changed and morphed into Madonna's single *Hollywood* – which was a hit at the time. Dressed in black, complete with a groom's top hat and tailcoat, Madonna came on stage to join her brides. After performing *Hollywood*, Madonna

INTRODUCTION

shed her formal wear to reveal a vest and elbow-length gloves beneath the jacket.

And then – in a move that guaranteed she would make headlines across the world the following day – the superstar kissed first Spears then Aguilera.

Once again, Madonna had proved that she is never entirely as she seems. In case there could be any doubt, Spears later confirmed the kiss was Madonna's idea, telling MTV News: "She threw the idea around a couple of times in rehearsal." Spears also stressed how she had always been a big fan of Madonna. She said: "The whole moment was so surreal because I've looked up to her and I sang *Like a Virgin* when I was three or four, so being up there was a moment that I will never, ever forget. It was a performance of a lifetime. Being in her presence was an honour."

The influence of Madonna on younger generations cannot be over-exaggerated. She has been constantly reinventing herself since she was a child, and her ability to shock even those who think they know better is both a tribute to her business skills and the reason behind her staying power. Only Madonna could flirt with two of the current crop of pop princesses in August and then successfully launch a children's book in

INTRODUCTION

September. In fact, only Madonna would even try.

Where others see limits, Madonna sees opportunity. In her 20-year career she has not just been a successful pop singer – she is one of the most successful female recording artist ever. She is also a movie star, businesswoman, stage actress, author, model and mother. Her iconic image changes inspire whole new generations of fans and performers – her influence on Spears and Aguilera's careers is easy to see, and both acknowledge her as a guiding light.

Madonna's is the story of the American Dream, that nothing is impossible. Sheer hard work, determination and talent have brought her to the position she occupies on today's A-List. She has ultimate control over her career, even holding a stake in the record company that releases her material.

Madonna's life is not easy to analyse because, whenever you feel you have reached an understanding, she does something that makes you rethink everything you thought you knew. To even attempt to understand Madonna's drive and passion, you must have a sense of what she has been through. Her mother's death when Madonna was very young certainly shaped her childhood, as did the strictly religious household in which she was raised. Looking back at the young Madonna's

INTRODUCTION

courage and drive, we see a woman who went to New York to further her career without knowing anyone in the city. Not only did she survive, she flourished in the Big Apple, meeting people who would help her career take flight. When it came to her performing career, Madonna started early and, fired with extraordinary ambition, became devoted to dance, music and drama.

But, of course, it was music that took her to the top first and has kept her there for more than 20 years. From her first hit *Holiday*, her musical journey is charted here, along with the videos that made Madonna much more than simply a dance-floor-filler. As Madonna's chameleon quality applies as much to her music as her image, her many influences and styles are documented, from the Boy Toy belts worn early in her career to the cowboy chic of the *Music* album.

Winning awards has become something of a regular occurrence for Madonna, she has been nominated for 61 MTV Video Music Awards and won Grammys, American Music Awards and Brit Awards to name but a few. And no look at Madonna's musical career would be complete without considering Maverick, her record company, which has produced all her albums since *Erotica* in 1992.

MADONNA

INTRODUCTION

However, from the beginning, Madonna has never limited herself to one career. As early as 1979 she appeared in movies, making the break into the big time with *Desperately Seeking Susan* in 1985, alongside Rosanna Arquette. Since then, Madonna has had to struggle to prove herself as an actress to the press, although her performance in *Evita* certainly made a lot of critics take notice. She has also performed on stage on both sides of the Atlantic, as well as making guest appearances on sitcoms such as her recent appearance on the hit series *Will and Grace*.

The film production arm of her record company, Maverick Entertainment Inc, also handles movies such as 2003's *Agent Cody Banks* and its 2004 sequel *Agent Cody Banks 2 – Destination London*. Featuring *Malcolm in the Middle* star Frankie Muniz, Hilary Duff and ex-S Club 7 performer Hannah Spearritt, these children's adventure films are very different from the movies Madonna makes as an actress. Maverick is also slated to be producing a 2005 remake of *Charlie and the Chocolate Factory* starring Johnny Depp.

Madonna is not someone who plays by the rules, and this makes her infinitely more interest-ing than most performers and, consequently, a

INTRODUCTION

media favourite. Sometimes it seems that there is nothing Madonna likes more than to shock her audience. From posing nude in a book about fantasies to swearing repeatedly on television, Madonna captures headlines better than anyone else. Her concerts and even her documentary *In Bed With Madonna* seem designed to provoke a reaction. Her videos have been banned from VH1 and MTV and she has been threatened with arrest for obscene behaviour on-stage.

Although she seems less publicity-hungry since the birth of her children, Madonna is still extremely skilled at demonstrating the shock factor, as her Spears/Aguilera MTV kiss proved. Madonna is a publicity queen who seems, not only to change her image at will, but also to control her own press image, making sure people see her the way she wishes to be seen.

The only area in her life where Madonna does not always appear to be in control is her romantic life. An early marriage did not work out, and was followed by numerous relationships with famous men – some of whom betrayed her trust – and some not-so-famous men who got tired of being labelled Mr Madonna. But, like anyone, there have been some men in her life – first husband Sean Penn,

MADONNA

INTRODUCTION

Carlos Leon, who fathered Madonna's first child Lourdes, and Guy Ritchie, father of Rocco, and Madonna's current husband. All have influenced her life and had an impact on her.

The arrival of Lourdes and Rocco has not dimmed Madonna's capacity to shock. However, there can be little doubt that today's Madonna is a calmer, more relaxed and spiritually focussed woman than she was before the birth of her children. They have influenced her professionally, from her writings to her musical style.

After enduring a strict Catholic upbringing – which she later rebelled against by wearing rosaries as jewellery and using religious imagery to controversial effect in her *Like a Prayer* video – Madonna is also devoted to the Kabbalah teachings, which inspired her to write two best-selling children's books.

Adding to the shift in the public's perception of her, Madonna's move to the United Kingdom to be with Guy Ritchie, has seen the previously all-American girl embracing the English country lifestyle, complete with mansion retreat.

Despite her new, quieter existence, controversy is still never far behind Madonna, often due to her outspoken nature, and in 2000 she upset many

MADONNA

INTRODUCTION

Brits by announcing on Kiss FM in Los Angeles that she would not have her baby in an English hospital because they were "old and Victorian". "Come on now," she said, "have you been to hospitals in England?" A few months later she made the news again when she complained that British workmen did not work as hard as their American counterparts, saying during a web chat with fans: "The work week [in Britain] starts at noon on Monday and ends at noon on Friday. I'm a bit spoiled – I'm used to people in America working seven days a week... There are bank holidays every minute here."

Still, despite the occasional quibble, which is probably less complaining than your average Brit, Madonna claims to love her life in the UK. Her husband now refers to her as "the missus" and she has been known to enjoy a drink or two in her local pub.

Madonna has true star quality. She always seems to know when to hold something back and how to keep her public wanting more. Whether that is something you are born with or something you develop, she has it in abundance and that is what is at the heart of her iconic presence.

The early years

MADONNA

THE EARLY YEARS

ll legends start somewhere and, although Bay City, Michigan, may seem an unlikely place, it is here that Madonna Louise Ciccone was born on 16 August 1958. She spent her early life here as part of a large Catholic family which suffered a terrible loss in 1963 when Madonna's mother died from breast cancer. In the difficult times that followed Madonna proved herself a survivor. She also proved that she had the energy, drive and ability to become a performer, taking up dance, and acting in high school plays as she got older. This drive and ambition marked the young Madonna as a future superstar.

MADONNA

THE EARLY YEARS

Madonna was named Madonna Louise after her mother. She later chose to add Veronica as her confirmation name, opting for the name of the woman who gave Jesus a handkerchief to wipe his brow when he was carrying the cross. Immediately nicknamed 'Little Nonni' to distinguish her from her mother, she was the first girl born to Silvio and Madonna Ciccone (née Fortin). Silvio – who later anglicised his name to Tony – was one of six boys born to Gaetano and Michelina Ciccone, who came to America from Italy in the Twenties. Silvio and Madonna were not well off and so had to show grit and perseverance when raising their young family and trying to make ends meet.

Madonna later said of her father in an interview: "My father is first-generation American... My grandmother and grandfather weren't very educated and I think in a way they represented a lifestyle that my father really didn't want to have anything to do with. It's not that he was ashamed, really, but he wanted to be better... I think he wanted us to have a better life than he did when he was growing up."

Sadly, though, Little Nonni's early life would be tragically overshadowed by the death of her mother when Madonna was only five-years-old. In

MADONNA

THE EARLY YEARS

1962 her mother was diagnosed with breast cancer when she was pregnant with her sixth child, Melanie. A devout Catholic, Madonna's mother sought comfort in her religion as her illness worsened. She died on 1 December 1963.

Her mother's illness and early death meant that Madonna took on a number of adult responsibilities in the household. She looked after her younger siblings, Paula, Christopher and Melanie. She later said: "I didn't feel close to anyone in my family when I was growing up... I didn't feel close to my older brothers, they were just typical older brothers who tortured me all the time."

Indeed Madonna would later tell many magazine journalists tales of what 'tortures' Anthony and Martin devised for their little sister – such as hanging her on the clothesline by her underpants. One can quite easily imagine the young Madonna's indignation at such treatment.

Her father wanted his children to do well at school and would offer each of them 50 cents for every 'A' they received on their report card. Much to her father's delight, Madonna proved to be a straight-A student. Even early in her life, Madonna always wanted to be the best.

MADONNA

THE EARLY YEARS

In 1966 Tony married Joan Gustafson, the housekeeper. Soon there were two more children in the house, with Jennifer and Mario arriving in 1967 and 1968. The now very large family moved to Rochester, Michigan – a place with plenty of small-town charm but which wouldn't have been very appealing to a young lady who was expected to leave her old life behind and start a new one in a new town, complete with a new mother figure. By all accounts this was a difficult transitional time for Madonna, who had grown quite used to being the woman of the house and the apple of her father's eye. She began to misbehave, disliking the fact that she was expected to wear the same clothes as her sisters. Even at the age of 10, Madonna wanted to stand out.

Unsurprisingly, some of Madonna's attention-seeking behaviour took place when she was given a public platform. At the St Andrews school talent show Little Nonni shocked her father by appearing on the stage in a tribute to Goldie Hawn's *Laugh-In* go-go dancer routine, dressed in a bikini and covered in fluorescent green paint, which made her look nude.

She later remembered that she was nearly naked – wanting to shock and outrage people so that

THE EARLY YEARS

they would remember her performance on the one year when it might be considered acceptable. Although the other parents gave the small performer a standing ovation, Tony was not impressed and grounded his daughter for two weeks.

As Madonna got older she harnessed her creative energy, taking dance lessons and appearing in high school shows. She performed with the Adams High Thespian Society in such plays as *My Fair Lady*, *The Adams Family*, *Cinderella* and *Godspell*. She was also a cheerleader for the Rochester Adams Highlanders.

At the age of 15 Madonna started dance classes with 42-year-old Christopher Flynn, who became one of the strongest influences on the young wannabe. Flynn was known for being fierce with his students, but he quickly developed a warm bond with Madonna and would take her to museums and art galleries. He also frequently took his student dancing in the trendy burgeoning gay disco scene of Downtown Detroit, opening up the youngster's eyes to alternate lifestyles that were a world away from the confines of her strict Catholic home life.

Needless to say, her father wasn't thrilled about these trips. However, he was very proud when Madonna, encouraged by Flynn, won a scholarship to study dance at the University of Michigan. It meant her leaving high school a semester early, but it also meant that his daughter was going to university. Flynn worked as a teacher on the course and so continued working with Madonna and her dancing talent.

Even in her teens, Madonna battled convention. In a class full of elegant ballerinas, Madonna wore torn leotards held together with safety pins, and had her hair black, short and spiky. She was making a fashion statement and at the same time she was asserting her individuality, proving she was different.

On the way...

ON THE WAY...

ndeed, Madonna did not stay long at the University of Michigan. Again with the support of her dance teacher Flynn, she got a place on a six-week summer course with the Alvin Ailey Dance Theatre in New York. Flynn then backed her up when she decided to drop out of her university course – even though she was not yet halfway through – to go to New York to take a chance at fulfiling what she believed to be her destiny. Even then Flynn recognised that Madonna's talent couldn't be contained by academic dance.

Flynn understood the young Madonna's

ambition and encouraged her to push herself. When Flynn died of Aids in 1990, Madonna was devastated, stating at the time that she had lost her mentor. Madonna has lost several other close friends to Aids, and has always been actively involved in fundraising and awareness work for the illness.

So, although her father disapproved of the idea – believing firmly in the importance of education – Madonna moved to New York, earning some of the money to do so by posing nude for art students for $10 an hour.

Legend then tells us that, when Madonna arrived in New York she carried nothing but a single suitcase and $37 cash. Upon hailing a cab at the airport she told the driver to take her "to the centre of everything". For a fee of $15 he took her to Times Square. Ten years later, at the premiere of her film *Who's That Girl?*, Madonna announced to the cheering crowd: "Ten summers ago I made my first trip to New York City. My first plane ride, my first cab ride. I didn't know where I was going, I didn't know a soul. And I told the taxi driver to drop me off in the middle of everything, so he dropped me off at Times Square. I was completely awestruck."

MADONNA

ON THE WAY...

Whether or not this tale is true, upon arriving in New York, Madonna had many part-time jobs — few of which lasted more than a couple of weeks — in places such as Dunkin' Donuts, the Russian Tea Room and Burger King. She also posed nude again, for the Art Students' League. Years later these nude pictures would return to haunt her.

For a brief time Madonna worked with Pearl Lang's dance company. Andrew Morton revealed in his biography, *Madonna* how Lang later summed up Madonna's talent: "I was fond of her arrogance, her hunger and her spunk. Nothing fazed her. She was going to do something and nothing was going to get in her way."

However, when Madonna realised that it would take five more years before she could be experienced enough to be accepted into a major touring dance company, she quit, telling Lang she'd decided to be a rock star.

Before the onset of rock stardom, Madonna moved to France and for a brief time in 1979 became part of European disco star Patrick Hernandez's act in Paris. While in Paris, promises were made to Madonna that she would soon become a disco star. Madonna later recalled that they tried to turn her into a Donna Summer-esque disco star, but she didn't want that. She returned to America within a couple of months.

Back in New York, Madonna began seeing a musician called Dan Gilroy, and she soon moved in with him and his brother Ed, who was also a performer. While staying with the brothers, she began writing songs and learning to play the guitar and drums. When Madonna discovered that one of her friends from dance class, Angie Smit, played bass guitar, the four decided to join forces, and became The Breakfast Club – so named because they used to rehearse all night and then go out for breakfast as day was dawning.

The Breakfast Club played a couple of gigs but things did not seem to get off the ground. Meanwhile, Madonna and Angie Smit took part in an erotic movie called *A Certain Sacrifice*. The movie was not finished at the time due to problems with the budget, and it was not released until 1985, by which time Madonna was world famous. This was not the only case of people releasing early material once she became well known – in 1980 Madonna also made some extra money performing backing vocals for an artist called Otto von Wernherr on his songs *Cosmic Club*, *We Are the*

ON THE WAY...

Gods, and *Wild Dancing*. These songs were not released until 1986.

With arguments about control causing the break-up of The Breakfast Club, Madonna formed another band, The Millionaires. This name was later changed to Emmy – band member Steve Bray's nickname for Madonna.

Despite enjoying more success with Emmy than she had with her previous bands, by 1981 Madonna was living off popcorn and seriously considering going back home. But just as she was beginning to despair, Emmy were offered a contract with Gotham Records, a result of Madonna's friendship with a music talent agent Camille Barbone. However, Madonna was beginning to feel restricted by life in a band, and had a burning desire to make it on her own.

Emmy split and after the break-up Madonna decided that she was the only one who was going to make her career happen, and she was not going to depend on anyone else to do it for her. She made a demo recording of four tracks – *Everybody*, *Stay*, *Burning Up* and *Ain't No Big Deal* – with her ex-boyfriend and ex-bandmate Steve Bray. She took the tracks to Mark Kamins, the DJ at trendsetting nightclub Danceteria, and persuaded him to play

ON THE WAY...

Everybody. Kamins was astonished at the reaction the track received and he took her track to Michael Rosenblatt at Sire Records.

In 1982 Madonna signed to Sire Records for a two-single deal. Her first American single, *Everybody*, was released in October 1982 and – although it did not make the all-important Billboard Top 100 singles chart – it climbed to number one in the dance charts. The follow-up to *Everybody* was *Burning Up*, and this track also made number one in the dance charts.

Realising that they had a potential star on their hands, Sire Records decided not to let Madonna slip away once her two-single deal was complete and swiftly signed her for an album deal. While looking for and recording songs for the new album, Madonna's boyfriend at the time John 'Jellybean' Benitez found a song he thought Madonna might like to record. Written by Curtis Hudson and Lisa Stevens, the song was *Holiday* and provided the young singer with her first hit in the British charts.

With the promise of an album deal, Madonna realised it was time to hire a manager. Relinquishing control like this was not easy for the headstrong young singer. But having made the decision, she was determined that the person she hired would be the best in the business. Freddy DeMann, of Weisner-DeMann Entertainment, was certainly one of the top entertainment managers at the time, handling Michael Jackson whose *Off the Wall* album had recently established him as a huge solo star. Co-founder of Sire Records, Seymour Stein, arranged a meeting, and DeMann agreed to handle Madonna.

Her first album, called simply *Madonna*, was a smash hit, making the American top 10 and spawning several hit singles. Produced by Reggie Lucas, it includes the hit songs, *Borderline*, *Holiday* and *Lucky Star*. The album spent an incredible 168 weeks in the The Billboard 200 chart in the US. Madonna wrote five out of the eight songs on the album, which has now sold over five million copies in the US alone. Madonna was fast on her way to becoming a celebrity. Right from the start, Madonna was an artist to be reckoned with.

Madonna was making her name in the music world. She still, however, had ambitions for other areas of the entertainment business. Many have remarked that Madonna's most remarkable characteristic is her ability to aim higher consistently, to never stop trying, In 1984 she said: "Three to four years ago dancing was the most important thing – now it's music. That will lead on to something else... acting. Above all, I want to be an all-round entertainer."

4

Music

MADONNA

MUSIC

rom pop to dance, from *Like A Virgin* to *Ray of Light*, Madonna has dabbled with many musical styles and produced records that find favour with a wide range of fans across the world. With more top 10 hits than The Beatles and Rolling Stones combined, she is without doubt the most prolific pop star of her generation.

She is the mother of musical reinvention and, over the years, she has written much of the music that has captivated the record-buying public herself. She's created music that has made it hard to pigeonhole her – her recordings have nodded in the direction of just about the full range of modern

MUSIC

musical genres. Perhaps most importantly, she's never been afraid to delve into her personal life when she's needed inspiration for her songs. To date, she has penned songs about her mother's death, her father's strictness and about how she felt when she became a mother for the first time. Her songs have covered serious social issues such as teenage pregnancy as well as altogether more frivolous issues such as the dance craze she popularised with the hit record *Vogue*. Madonna has produced chart-topping dance records and, ever the pop chameleon, she has even successfully tried her hand at rapping.

Although she has proved she can excel as an actress, a dancer and even an author of children's books, chances are that Madonna will always be best known for her music. And when it comes to making music, Madonna has proved that whatever she puts her mind to, she's got what it takes. Ever since January 1984, when the single *Holiday* became her first UK hit, she's enjoyed two decades of unmatched success.

Holiday reached number six in the British singles chart. The follow-up single, *Lucky Star*, reached a respectable number 14. However, the record that came next, *Borderline*, only managed

MUSIC

to get to number 56. It's hard to believe now, but despite enjoying continued success in the USA, it looked for a while as if young Madonna would leave the UK music scene with the same speed as when she'd arrived only a few months earlier.

Then came *Like A Virgin*. Complete with shocking lyrics and a controversial appearance on the first MTV Video Music Awards in 1984 – where the singer dressed as a bride and writhed around on top of a huge wedding cake – *Like A Virgin* went to number three in the UK, number one in the US and became a worldwide hit, notching up sales of 2.25 million in the process. *Borderline* and *Holiday* were subsequently re-released, both reaching number two on their second run in the UK charts. Other singles from the *Like A Virgin* album also did well, such as *Material Girl* (number three), *Angel* (number five) and *Into the Groove* which in July 1985 gave Madonna her first UK number one. It was to be the first of many – Madonna has had more UK number one singles and albums than any other female solo artist.

Like A Virgin spawned the 1985 Virgin Tour. Despite being a relative newcomer to the music scene she was already performing in some of the world's most prestigious venues. At New York's Radio City Music Hall she sold more than 17,500 tickets in 34 minutes, setting a record for the fastest sell-out. Many acts wanted to support the woman who had quickly become one of pop's hottest properties, that honour eventually went to cheeky white rappers the Beastie Boys who were causing something of a stir in the music world themselves. Her global appeal was further demonstrated in 1985 when she was asked to be part of the American line-up for the huge Live Aid concert.

The video for *Material Girl* featured Madonna dressing in the same style as Marilyn Monroe when she sang *Diamonds Are A Girl's Best Friend* in the film *Gentlemen Prefer Blondes*. Through the years Madonna's fondness for the stars of yesteryear, including Rita Hayworth and Marlene Dietrich, and Monroe in particular, has frequently resurfaced in her work. For the MTV generation the video has become something of a classic. For Madonna it was memorable for another reason – it was on this shoot that Madonna first met her future husband, actor Sean Penn.

Around the mid-Eighties Madonna's style, musically, was in the mainstream dance/pop mould. However, her dress style was something new. Fingerless lace gloves, bed hair, chunky jewellery, crucifixes and Boy Toy belts soon found their way into the wardrobes of young girls everywhere. Young girls were copying her in their droves, but at the same time as they were doing all they could to follow her lead, she was searching for a new look. Madonna seemed to realise early on that, by constantly changing her image, she could secure her place as a trendsetter and always stay ahead of her contemporaries.

Her hair went from long and blonde to short and platinum for the video for *Papa Don't Preach* in 1986, a song which caused quite a fuss in some sectors of the American press. Some conservative commentators believed that the lyrics – about a young girl confessing to her father that she is pregnant and wants to keep the child – were pro-life. Others said that the song encouraged sex before marriage. Whatever the truth behind the song was, each news story about Madonna simply made her more famous. And they didn't hurt her record sales either, both *Papa Don't Preach*, with its catchy chorus, and its follow-up *True Blue* went to number one. *Papa Don't Preach* also won Madonna her first MTV Music Video Award for Best Female Video.

MADONNA

MUSIC

From wearing an "Italians do it better" top in the *Papa Don't Preach* video, Madonna then went Spanish with *La Isla Bonita* – another number one. The song was a deviation from her music style up to that point, featuring Spanish-style guitars and a video in which Madonna dressed as a flamenco dancer. Her practice of borrowing from other cultures had begun. As had her extremely successful habit of recording songs from films, her fifth British number one was *Who's That Girl?* from her 1987 film of the same name. Madonna's *Who's That Girl?* World Tour came to London in August 1987, where 144,000 tickets were sold in 18 hours for two sell-out Wembley Stadium shows.

In 1989 Madonna released the album *Like A Prayer*. This heralded the beginning of a new, more controversial phase in her music career. Her video for *Like A Prayer* had religious groups up in arms with its portrayal of burning crosses and a black Jesus. Madonna, her hair dark brown for the video, glided through the fuss pretty much unscathed. Although she lost her advertising deal with Pepsi, *Like A Prayer* provided Madonna with another number one hit on both sides of the Atlantic and the MTV Music Video Viewers' Choice Award.

Other top five hits from the same album were

MUSIC

Express Yourself, *Cherish* and *Dear Jessie*. While the video for *Cherish* was family friendly – a black-and white affair directed by the high-profile and ultra-cool photographer Herb Ritts, and featuring Madonna on a beach with mermaids – *Express Yourself* was something else entirely. A celebration of the male body beautiful, the video also featured Madonna naked and in chains. The video won several MTV Video Music Awards, including Best Direction and Best Cinematography, while the single climbed to number five in the UK charts.

Madonna's Blonde Ambition World Tour came to the UK in July 1990. Featured in her documentary *In Bed With Madonna*, this was one of her most newsworthy outings, with cities threatening cancellations due to the show's lewd nature. *Rolling Stone* magazine called it: "A nifty summation of the spectacle that is Madonna."

Vogue remains one of Madonna's most enduring successes, hitting the top spot in both the US and the UK. The video, directed by David Fincher, was again stylishly filmed in black and white and features Madonna reeling off the names of those stars of the past who have inspired her – stars like Grace Kelly, James Dean and baseball player Joe DiMaggio. Classic and classy, the *Vogue*

MUSIC

video dominated the 1990 MTV Video Music Awards, triumphing in the Best Direction, Best Editing and Best Cinematography categories, as well as winning the Viewers' Choice Award. Madonna also gave a sassy live performance of *Vogue* at the awards wearing an Elizabethan-style costume, complete with wig, fan and hooped skirt, which was raised at times to give the audience a glimpse of her underwear. The performance was extremely sexy, with dancers grabbing at various parts of the singer's anatomy, and the audience loved it, whooping and hollering their approval as Madonna was carried off the stage on a chaise lounge held aloft by her male dancers.

Vogue was taken from the album that accompanied Madonna's 1990 movie *Dick Tracy*. Called *I'm Breathless* – a reference to her character in the film, Breathless Mahoney – much of the material on the album was inspired by the Forties-feel of the film, however the mischievous side of Madonna also had a look in. *Hanky Panky* – a cheeky, kinky song in praise of spanking – was released as a single in July 1990 and reached number two, only being kept off the top spot by *Turtle Power*, a little-remembered novelty record by an act called Partners in Kryme.

MADONNA

In 1990 she released *The Immaculate Collection*, an album featuring her greatest hits to date. It has sold over 22 million copies worldwide, more than 3.3 million in the UK alone. Past hits, such as *Like A Virgin*, *Papa Don't Preach* and *Express Yourself* were included, as were two new singles *Rescue Me* and *Justify My Love* - which both reached number two on the charts.

However, *Justify My Love* – with seductive whispering making up much of the single – was not appreciated merely for its musical properties, but also for its raunchy video, which was banned from MTV and VH1 for explicit sexual content. Directed by Jean Baptiste Mondino and shot in a Paris hotel, the video features Madonna exploring her sexual fantasies with many different characters. The song was co-written by Madonna, Lenny Kravitz and Ingrid Cesares and was a huge worldwide hit, selling over 3 million copies.

5

Stetsons off

MADONNA

n 1992 Madonna toyed with her femininity and sexuality in the book *Sex* and the album *Erotica*. The book in particular caused a big fuss in the press. As usual, all the publicity did Madonna no harm whatsoever, and all the singles from *Erotica* – *Deeper and Deeper*, *Bad Girl*, *Erotica*, *Fever* and *Rain* – made it into the British top ten.

The video for *Bad Girl* saw a blonde-haired Madonna paired up with Hollywood actor Christopher Walken, while the video for *Rain* featured her looking elfin and stunning, with a short black wig and bright blue eyes. The MTV voters once again awarded Madonna some of their top prizes, voting *Rain* the winner in the Best Art Direction and Best Cinematography categories.

But perhaps more shocking in 1992 than Madonna's display of overt sexuality was her decision to cover up everything in a floral print dress and record the ballad *This Used To Be My Playground* for the soundtrack of the family film she was appearing in, *A League of Their Own*. Fans of Madonna, who thought they were immune to her attempts to shock, were caught out by this image change. *This Used To Be My Playground* was also a huge hit, peaking at number three in the charts.

Erotica was also the first of Madonna's albums to be produced by her own record company, Maverick. Funded by Warner Bros – who also own Sire Records, the label all Madonna's previous work had been released on – Maverick was launched in the early Nineties. At the time Madonna said of the venture: "My goal is to have hits with the company. I'm not one of those dumb artists who is just given a label to shut her up." And she has proved the truth behind this statement, signing Alanis Morrissette to the label, whose album *Jagged Little Pill* sold nearly 30 million copies after its release in 2000. Proving Madonna's savvy as a business woman, Maverick later went on to produce films as well.

The Girlie Show World Tour kicked off at London's Wembley Stadium in September 1993. A review of the tour in *The New Yorker* said: "Her stage performance... is a wonder of our times." The tour needed 1,500 costumes for Madonna and her dancers and created headlines throughout the world.

By now, Madonna had been producing hits for 10 years. With her 1984 album *Bedtime Stories* the multi-talented singer merged her sexy side with her softer side, producing yet more memorable songs and videos along the way. Her softer side was evident in the beautiful ballad *Take A Bow*, the video for which had the Spanish flavour previously seen in *La Isla Bonita*, and saw Madonna's heart being broken by a matador.

Sexuality was the focus of the song *Human Nature*, directed by Jean Baptiste Mondino (the director responsible for the controversial *Justify My Love* video). This video featured Madonna and her dancers in black PVC, the singer sporting black corn-rowed hair and a ton of attitude as she spits out lyrics at the camera. Dominatrix images give the video the edge favoured by both Mondino and Madonna, while the choreography fully showcases Madonna's talents as a dancer. The vocals were also unlike anything Madonna had done before, with an unusual nasal quality to her voice which complemented the style of the song and helped it reach number eight in the UK chart.

The 1996 movie *Evita* produced several hit singles for Madonna, all of which appeared on a soundtrack album which sold 11 million copies worldwide. The singles were *You Must Love Me*, *Don't Cry For Me Argentina* and *Another Suitcase in Another Hall*, released between late 1996 and early 1997. All made the top 10 but none hit the top spot. It was now nearly seven years since Madonna had produced a UK number one, although *Justify My Love*, *This Used To Be My Playground* and *Take A Bow* had all gone to the top of the charts in America.

A year went by without a new Madonna single. Then, in March 1998 came *Frozen*. Taken from the Grammy Award-winning album *Ray of Light*, *Frozen* went straight into the charts at number one, the first of her singles to do so. The video was a masterpiece of computer image work – winning the MTV Music Video Award for Best

MADONNA

STETSONS OFF

Special Effects – with a black-haired, black-robed Madonna turning into a flock of ravens. This video also introduced fans to Madonna's new Indian-inspired image, reflected in her dance moves and henna-tattooed hand. Now a mother, Madonna had gone through yet another successful image change.

Drowned World (Substitute For Love) was certainly a more mature recording, with Madonna addressing fame and choices, ending the video embracing a dark haired girl – who represents, but is not, Madonna's daughter Lourdes. When Madonna hugs the child she says: "This is my religion," possibly commenting on her new priorities since the birth of her daughter Lourdes.

Two more movie tie-in singles proved big hits for Madonna in 1999 and 2000. First there was *Beautiful Stranger*, taken from the soundtrack to the movie *Austin Powers – The Spy Who Shagged Me*, which got to number two and spent 16 weeks on the charts. The video showed Madonna with the actor Mike Myers, in character as Austin Powers, and the catchy tune was one of the standout hits of the summer of 1999.

American Pie – Madonna's cover of the Don McLean classic – went straight to the top spot in March 2000. Taken from *The Next Best Thing,*

STETSONS OFF

Madonna's movie with Rupert Everett. Everett, who as well as being her co-star is a close friend of Madonna's, also featured in the video.

The time had come for another album and in 2000 Madonna released *Music*. The single of the same name, released on 2 September 2000, went straight to number one in the UK, and also hit the top of the charts in America. It went on to sell 3.5 million copies worldwide, making it Madonna's third bestselling single, behind *Like A Prayer* (4.2 million) and *Vogue* (5.9 million).

The video for *Music* – directed by Jonas Akerlund, featured Madonna adopting a whole new style, the cowboy look. She carried the look through to her next video which was for the single *Don't Tell Me*, directed again by Jean Baptiste Mondino. Soon Stetsons were perched on fashionable heads everywhere and Madonna was enjoying being back in the music spotlight. The birth of her son, Rocco, in August 2000 and her wedding to film director Guy Ritchie in December of the same year meant her name and face were hardly ever out of the papers. Her music, meanwhile, carried on selling in its millions.

Ritchie put his directorial talents to use on the video for the third single from *Music*, *What it*

STETSONS OFF

Feels Like For a Girl. Featuring an angry woman going on a crime spree, it was banned from MTV and VH1 in the USA for excessive violence. In the UK it was announced that the video would be shown on MTV, but only after midnight.

Madonna's Drowned World Tour played Earl's Court in July of 2001, and she became a Bond girl of sorts with a cameo in *Die Another Day*, and a single of the same name released in 2002, which reached number three in the charts. An extremely high-tech video appeared to show Madonna fencing with herself.

The second volume of her greatest hits, *GHV2*, was released in 2001. Although not as popular as *The Immaculate Collection*, *GHV2* still sold an impressive seven million copies worldwide. Singles such as *Erotica*, *Ray of Light* and *Music* were all featured.

American Life, the single taken from the album of the same name, was released in 2003. By this time, Madonna had settled in England with her husband and family and become a self-confessed Anglophile. The album conveyed a strong anti-war, anti-fashiion and anti-materialism sentiment – a comment on the negative aspects of American Life. The original video for the single, made before the conflict in Iraq began, was changed because Madonna felt it 'inappropriate' when her home country was at war. The single and its equally US-themed follow-up, *Hollywood*, both got to number two in the UK charts. *Hollywood* was also used in adverts Madonna made at the time for Gap with Missy Elliott. The album went straight to number one.

Madonna proved that she could still shock the establishment when she kissed both Britney Spears and Christina Aguilera at the MTV Video Music Awards in 2003. Prior to this she had started a trend for slogan T-shirts, sporting ones emblazoned with her husband's latest film, her children's names, and the name of fellow pop singer, Kylie Minogue.

Madonna and Britney Spears nearly kissed again in the video for their duet *Me Against the Music*, neatly capitalising on the publicity they had created at the MTV Video Music Awards. Onlookers observed that both Spears and Christina Aguilera have learned a lot about self-publicising and creating controversy from Madonna, and Madonna has spoken about her support for younger artists, such as Spears.

During her time on the charts, Madonna has

STETSONS OFF

been a Boy Toy, a Material Girl, a sex kitten and a dominatrix. She has worn the clothing of cultures from around the globe, and had her hair in many different styles and colours. When her Reinvention Tour was announced – with a publicity shot of the 45-year-old star wearing a blonde Marie-Antoinette-style wig – it seemed that the tour's title could not have been more appropriate. But whatever she wears and whatever controversy she creates, her music is always fresh and different.

Movies

MOVIES

adonna's movie career began in the late Seventies. Since then, she has smouldered as a showgirl and stripped for scenes of seduction. She has also played a missionary nurse and the iconic Eva Peron. It seems that, just as we cannot pigeon-hole Madonna's style or music, nor can we easily find what could be defined as a 'typical' Madonna role.

She landed her first acting part in 1979. She replied to an advert she'd seen in *Back Stage* magazine that was asking for "a dark fiery woman, dominant, with lots of energy, who can dance and is willing to work for no pay". Her response to the ad, placed by director Stephen Jon Lewicki, led to

MOVIES

her playing Bruna, a dominatrix, in the erotic film *A Certain Sacrifice*. Due to budgeting problems, the film was not released until 1985, by which time Madonna was a worldwide star. At the time, Madonna made an unsuccessful attempt to stop the film being released.

The fact that she responded to this particular advert says a lot about Madonna pre-stardom. New York has never been a cheap city in which to live. Madonna was earning paltry amounts singing in bands and posing for life artists. She really couldn't afford to appear in a movie for free but she wasn't going to let her financial situation hold her back. Madonna was determined to be a star and if she needed to work for free and play a dominatrix in order to get noticed, then so be it. There were no guarantees that the film would come out, and it was never going to be a blockbusting smash hit, but for the aspiring star, every chance, no matter how small, had to be taken.

Another of Madonna's early cinematic appearances was in *Crazy For You*, which was filmed in 1983. She appeared as a club singer, performing the title song plus another track called *Gambler*. Eventually released in 1985 with the title *Vision Quest* in America, this film was another that cashed in on Madonna's rapidly rising star status rather than helping her climb the precarious showbiz ladder. The film did have its uses, though. It is said that although brief, her performance in *Crazy For You* helped her win the title role in her first major mainstream film *Desperately Seeking Susan*.

Madonna was not the only person with an eye on the role of Susan – a street-smart free spirit. Leading young actresses of the day including Melanie Griffith, Jennifer Jason Leigh and Ellen Barkin were all considered for the part. Diane Keaton and Goldie Hawn were suggested for the two main parts, those of Susan and Roberta Glass, but director Susan Seidelman only had a budget of $5 million, plus she wanted to work with up-and-coming actors.

So it was Rosanna Arquette who won the Roberta Glass role, the New Jersey housewife who is married to a hot tub salesman but dreams of better things, and becomes obsessed with Madonna's character and aspires to be more like her. Referring to the character she played in the film, Madonna said at the time: "She has no roots, she represents freedom and adventure and all the things that normal people think they can't do."

MOVIES

At the time Madonna was filming *Desperately Seeking Susan*, she was becoming more and more famous as a hotshot singing sensation. People began to refer to *Desperately Seeking Susan* as "the Madonna movie". One of her songs, *Into the Groove*, was worked into the script to take advantage of her new-found popularity. *Desperately Seeking Susan* – a comic tale of mistaken identity and mishaps – did very well at the box office, earning $27.4 million in America alone, making "the Madonna movie" one of the top five grossing films of 1985.

1985 was a busy year for Madonna. As well as enjoying astonishing success with her music and film careers, she also found time to marry actor Sean Penn. The following year the two announced that they were going to make a film entitled *Shanghai Surprise* together. And as if the idea of Madonna and Penn appearing on-screen together was not tantalising enough for the press, the movie's executive producer was ex-Beatle George Harrison.

Advertised as 'a romantic adventure for the dangerous at heart', *Shanghai Surprise* was similar in style to the popular Indiana Jones movies and featured a romance between Madonna's missionary nurse and Penn's fortune-

MOVIES

hunter. Directed by Jim Goddard, the picture was beautiful to watch, having been filmed on location in Hong Kong. However, Madonna did not enjoy being on set, remembering that it was miserable at the time.

Madonna chose a comedy for her next movie, 1987's *Who's That Girl?* By now she was a huge star so when she told the film's producers that she wanted James Foley - who had directed her *Papa Don't Preach* and *Live to Tell* videos - to direct this film, they went along with her wishes. Legendary actor Sir John Mills appeared in a supporting role.

Madonna played Nikki Finn, a woman who, on her release from prison for a crime she did not commit, sets out to find the man who framed her. After playing a missionary nurse in *Shanghai Surprise*, this was a return to more familiar territory for Madonna. Like Susan in *Desperately Seeking Susan*, Nikki Finn was sexy, sassy, street-wise, modern young woman. *Who's That Girl?* also provided Madonna with a number one single on both sides of the Atlantic, as well as a top-selling album and sell-out tour, proving Madonna's musical stardom could benefit from her movie career and vice versa.

In the 1989 film *Bloodhounds of Broadway*,

she co-starred with *Dirty Dancing*'s Jennifer Grey and played a Twenties' showgirl. Grey took singing lessons so she could perform with confidence alongside Madonna in the movie, while Madonna herself took inspiration from the silent movie star Louise Brooks to create Hortense Hathaway, a character with a strong sexuality that sizzled on the screen. Sadly the director of *Bloodhounds of Broadway*, Howard Brookner, was suffering from Aids and died shortly after the movie was released. Madonna supported him by visiting him in hospital, where she also visited the other patients on the Aids ward. Her mentor during her early dancing years, Christopher Flynn, was also to die of the disease in 1990. Madonna remains a strong supporter of Aids charities.

One of Madonna's best performances came in 1990 when she appeared as Breathless Mahoney in the film *Dick Tracy*. Directed by and starring veteran actor Warren Beatty, the cast featured Al Pacino, Gene Hackman, Dustin Hoffman, Kathy Bates and James Caan. Madonna was in great company, although she admitted at a press conference for the movie that she had originally feared that she would have a problem with Beatty's way of working – which included a reputation for pushing his actors to 20 or 30 takes in his quest for the perfect scene.

Madonna was worried that her friendship with Beatty might cause problems if he tried to tell her what to do, but she found that she respected his judgement as he had been in the business for so many years.

The friendship Madonna referred to turned out to be more than just that. The two had a relationship that lasted throughout the filming and promotional period of *Dick Tracy* and in her documentary *In Bed With Madonna*, no secret is made of the fact that the *Dick Tracy* co-stars were a couple.

Madonna's character in *Dick Tracy* was a sultry singer and gangster's moll, who tries to come between Dick Tracy (Beatty) and his goody-goody girlfriend Tess Trueheart. As Mahoney, Madonna got to sing several show tunes written for the film by Stephen Sondheim, such as the ballad *Sooner or Later*, a song she included on her album *I'm Breathless*.

When awards time rolled around, *Dick Tracy* garnered a slew of nominations, especially in the field of make-up. The film won three Oscars, including the Best Song Oscar for *Sooner Or Later*.

MOVIES

Dressed in white and dazzling in diamonds, Madonna performed the song at the Oscar ceremony, where her companion for the evening was Michael Jackson.

Spotlight on... Desperately Seeking Susan

Now seen as a classic Eighties' movie, 1985's *Desperately Seeking Susan* was seen by many as the film that made Madonna an actress.

The style of the film is typical of the period, with both female leads – Madonna (Susan) and Rosanna Arquette (Roberta Glass) – sporting back-combed hair, lots of costume jewellery and heavy make-up. Lacey tops, large hair bows and bare midriffs also feature prominantly.

Madonna's co-star, Rosanna Arquette, had already appeared in several TV movies and shows, as well as being part of the Arquette acting dynesty, which also includes her siblings Alexis, David, Richmond and Patricia. Since her appearance in *Desperately Seeking Susan*, however, her career has gone from strength to strength, and she has enjoyed appearing in such films as *The Whole Nine Yards*, *Pulp Fiction* and the forthcoming *Kids in America*.

MADONNA

MOVIES

Director Susan Seidelman has enjoyed mixed success since 1985. High points include directing and producing *She-Devil* with Meryl Streep and Roseanne Barr, as well as grabbing a bit of television history by directing the pilot episode of *Sex and the City*.

Another famous name linked with the film – and an interesting bit of trivia – is Bruce Willis, who auditioned for the role of Madonna's boyfriend. The part eventually went to Robert Joy. Willis went on to appear in the television series *Moonlighting* that same year, and was appearing in blockbusters such as *Die Hard* by 1988.

7

In a league of her own

MADONNA

IN A LEAGUE OF HER OWN

adonna made two films in 1992 – *Shadows and Fog* and *A League of Their Own*. Her role in Woody Allen's *Shadows and Fog*, as a circus performer, was a very brief part in an all-star movie, which included Mia Farrow, John Malkovich, Jodie Foster and Kathy Bates.

A League of Their Own tells the story of a women's baseball team during the Second World War. It featured strong lead characters played by Tom Hanks and Geena Davis. As well as a supporting cast that included Rosie O'Donnell, Bill Pullman and Lori Petty. Madonna played 'All-the-Way' Mae Mordabito, 'All-the-Way' referring to her baseball skills, as well as her skill with the opposite sex! Mae was a great role for Madonna, once again sassy and sexy, backed with a steely determination and a fighting spirit.

A League of Their Own was a box office success. For Madonna it produced a top 10 single in the form of *This Used To Be My Playground*. She also came away from the film with a great friend in her co-star Rosie O'Donnell, and a much-appreciated recommendation from director Penny Marshall. When the producers for *Evita* were considering Madonna for the lead role they had some concerns that they would encounter diva-like behaviour. They contacted Marshall to enquire whether or not this was the case. Marshall's praise and a glowing reference helped reassure them, and Madonna was given the role.

Before *Evita*, however, Madonna was to appear in five more films. In the first two of these, *Dangerous Game* (also known as *Snake Eyes*) and *Body of Evidence*, Madonna once again demonstrated that her supreme confidence in her sexuality could be used to good effect on-screen.

Dangerous Game was produced by Maverick Picture Company, the movie-making spin-off of the music company Madonna set up in the early

MADONNA

Nineties. It starred Harvey Keitel and James Russo, and was directed by Abel Ferrara. A film about making a film, Keitel plays the director who pushes his stars Sarah Jennings and Francis Burns (Madonna and Russo) so hard that the relationship that disintegrates in the film is mirrored in their personal lives.

Body of Evidence sees Madonna as Rebecca Carlson, a woman accused of murdering her lover when he is found tied up with cocaine in his system and it is discovered that he's left Rebecca millions of dollars in his will. Willem Dafoe plays the lawyer brought in to represent Madonna's character in court. Before long, the lawyer and his client embark on a steamy affair, with plenty of kinky sex scenes – including one with candle wax which is now somewhat legendary!

Madonna's penchant for exploring sexuality through her work was at its peak in the early Nineties. As well as *Dangerous Game* and *Body of Evidence*, she also released of the book *Sex* and made sexually charged videos to accompany the singles *Erotica* and *Justify My Love*. Madonna has always been sexy. The new, even sexier Madonna was nominated for an MTV Movie Award for Most Desirable Female in recognition of her steamy performance in *Body of Evidence*.

Other smaller roles followed, such as a singing telegram in *Blue in the Face* (1995) and in Spike Lee's *Girl 6* (1996), where she had a cameo as the owner of a phone sex line.

Her role as Elspeth in the 'Missing Ingredient' segment of *Four Rooms* cast Madonna as an extremely sexy witch, who needs help from a bellboy (played by Tim Roth) to bring someone back from the dead. The film is comprised of four segments, each with its own storyline, the link between them provided by Roth's character.

Looking back, it's fair to say that most of Madonna's roles until 1996 shared certain characteristics. Almost all of the characters were sexy and street-smart, most were modern women with a modern mindset, who believed – as Madonna herself does – that women were men's equals. Also, all her roles so far had been fictional characters, so Madonna was free to interpret them in her own way. This was all to change when she took on the challenging role of Eva Peron in the musical *Evita*.

Madonna had wanted the role of Eva 'Evita' Peron ever since hearing that Alan Parker wanted to make a film version of the successful stage show. Here was another woman who had risen

IN A LEAGUE OF HER OWN

from the ordinary to be considered an icon and an inspiration. Madonna could certainly identify with aspects of Evita's personality, such as her courage, determination and perseverance. Plus the role was almost entirely singing. She must have felt as if the role was made for her.

However, she was not the only actress or singer with an eye on the prize. Among the names bandied about in the press as possible Eva Perons were Glenn Close, Bette Midler, Meryl Streep, Mariah Carey, Olivia Newton-John, Gloria Estefan, Liza Minnelli, Barbra Streisand and Michelle Pfeiffer. Of all of these, Pfeiffer got the closest to the movie, but she turned the role down, choosing to spend time with her young family, having been made aware of *Evita*'s busy shooting schedule. With perfect timing, just as Pfeiffer was saying no, Madonna wrote a letter to Alan Parker, asking him to let her have the part. It worked.

Madonna then worked extremely hard to improve her singing, broadening her range and vocal strength. The entire score was recorded before the actors – including fellow stars Antonio Banderas and Jonathan Pryce – went before the cameras. When filming began in Buenos Aires, Madonna threw herself into the role. She believed that the heat and punishing schedule was making her unwell and nauseous, but she battled on. What she would not find out until later was that at the time she was pregnant with her first child, Lourdes.

As a stage musical, *Evita* had been a smash hit for its authors Andrew Lloyd Webber and Tim Rice and so a lot was expected from the final film. Madonna had a lot of people to convince, particularly many Argentineans who did not believe the controversial singer should be playing someone they still regarded as saint-like.

Not only did Madonna convince everyone she was more than right for the part, she blew them away by becoming Evita on-screen. Her improved vocals impressed all and her gutsy performance won over the critics, particularly her rendition of *Don't Cry For Me Argentina*. Madonna had taken on the most challenging role of her career and, not only had she succeeded, she won the Golden Globe for Best Performance by an Actress in a Motion Picture (Musical/Comedy).

Aside from her 1999 song *Beautiful Stranger*, recorded as part of the soundtrack to the movie *Austin Powers – The Spy Who Shagged Me*, Madonna concentrated on music rather than movies between 1997 and 2000. It was her friend

IN A LEAGUE OF HER OWN

Rupert Everett who tempted her back to the big screen showing her a script for *The Next Best Thing*.

Abbie Reynolds, the character Madonna plays in *The Next Best Thing*, is a straight woman who has a one-night stand with her gay male best friend (played by Everett), and becomes pregnant by him. They raise the child together and are happy as an unconventional family, until Madonna's character falls for Ben Cooper (played by Benjamin Bratt) and a battle for the child begins.

Originally Abbie was written as a swimming instructor, but Madonna requested that it be changed to a yoga instructor as she felt it a more fitting occupation for the character. This may sound like a small change but it is an indication of how seriously Madonna takes her characterisation and performance in the films she has made. *The Next Best Thing* also gave Madonna her smash hit *American Pie*, with Everett appearing in the video.

In 2000 Madonna married director Guy Ritchie, who was responsible for such films as *Lock, Stock and Two Smoking Barrels* and *Snatch*. Husband and wife worked together on Madonna's 2001 video for *What It Feels Like For a Girl*, and on a BMW promotional film *The Hire: Star*. In 2002 they began working together on a full-length

IN A LEAGUE OF HER OWN

feature film, a remake of a 1974 Italian film *Travolti da un Insolito Destino Nell'Azzurro Mare d'Agosto*. Scripted by Ritchie and co-starring Adriano Giannini – playing the same role his father, Giancarlo Giannini had played in the original – the movie was called *Swept Away*.

The story of a spoilt woman shipwrecked on a desert island with a man she considers beneath her was filmed on location in Italy and Malta. Consequently the film is stunning to look at, a very different approach from Ritchie's previous gritty, realistic style of filming.

The film was not a hit with the critics. The press berated Madonna, claiming that she could not act and should stick to her singing. This seemed an unusually harsh criticism for an actress who had won the Golden Globe five years earlier. But the movie critics have always had trouble accepting Madonna as an actress, possibly because no matter how good her personality, she is so well known that they find it hard to forget that they are watching Madonna. Other singers – such as Mariah Carey, Britney Spears and Jennifer Lopez – have found it equally hard to be taken seriously in their film careers.

Audiences for both *Up For Grabs* (her 2002

MADONNA

IN A LEAGUE OF HER OWN

West End debut) and *Speed the Plow* (Madonna's 1988 Broadway appearance) have commented on the fact that you can never switch off your awareness that you are watching Madonna.

Peter Hepple, of *The Stage* newspaper, referred to this in his review of Madonna's performance in *Up For Grabs.* He said: "Certainly the star is the main reason for going to see it, and whatever one might guiltily wish, Madonna is not bad at all."

But despite an often harsh critical response to her cinematic appearances, Madonna keeps going and, to date, she has made some great films and delivered some really strong performances, all the time maintaining her stellar singing career. As if this were not enough, she has also been a movie producer, taking a behind-the-scenes role on the hit children's film *Agent Cody Banks* and its sequel. It looks like she enjoys this less visible role – projects announced for 2004/5 already include the forthcoming movies *She Rocks*, *Chasing Fate* and *This Is America*.

A powerful player by anyone's standards, Madonna's filmography is an impressive tribute to a very determined and focussed actress.

8

Mischief

Madonna burst on to the UK music scene with her first hit 'Holiday' in 1984. She has had numerous hits over the past 20 years and with each new hit comes a new image, if anyone can define the word 'reinvention' it is Madonna.

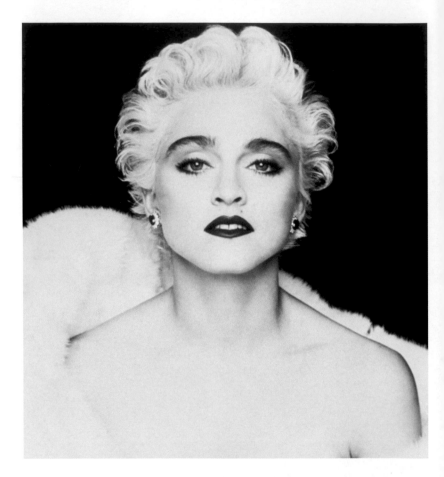

Winning awards is a regular occurance for Madonna, she has been nominated for 61 MTV Video Music Awards and won Grammys, American Music Awards and Brit Awards to name but a few. Although not limiting herself to a music career she has also excelled as an actress winning a Golden Globe for her performance as Eva Peron in 'Evita'.

Madonna and British director Guy Ritchie met at a party in 1998, they married in December 2000 at Skibo Castle, Scotland and have settled in the UK.

Not only is Madonna a singer, movie star and stage actress she is also a published author. Here she is pictured with her daughter, Lourdes, and her son, Rocco at the launch party for her book entitled 'The Little Roses' (London, September 2003).

MADONNA

MISCHIEF

ausing a Commotion is not only the title of one of Madonna's many top 10 hits, it is also one of her most prominent skills. She has the ability to whip the press into a frenzy over her latest project – be it music, a movie, a video or a book. The woman with the ever-changing image certainly knows how to get people talking. Many times she has done this through the quality of her music alone, yet at other times she has deliberately pushed the boundaries further than anyone else before her: riding the wave of publicity she's cleverly orchestrated; leaving controversy and debate in her wake.

MADONNA

MISCHIEF

She started early. Her image in 1984, at the time of *Like A Virgin*, caused a wave of concern when young girls began to copy her style. Crucifixes were the accessories of choice for the wannabes. Bellybuttons were bared. However, when Madonna was asked about her responsibility to those who looked up to her, she said: "That's a tough question. Because in a way my first response is: "I don't have a responsibility to them. They decided to look up to me, or use me as a role model. My only responsibility, I think, is to be true to myself."

In 1996 some critics claimed that the lyrics of *Papa Don't Preach* were enticing young women into sex before marriage. Madonna answered her critics in the press. Speaking of the song's main character, she said: "She has a very close relationship with her father and wants to maintain that closeness. To me it's a celebration of life. It says, 'I love you, father, and I love this man and this child that is growing inside me.'"

At times, her videos rather than the songs are the cause of all the commotion in the press. Particularly notable for the amount of fuss they caused were the videos for *Like A Prayer* (1989), *Justify My Love* (1990), *Erotica* (1992), and *What*

MISCHIEF

it Feels Like For a Girl (2001). Whether it's religious imagery, sexual fantasies or excessive violence, Madonna has tipped the scales with these videos and got everybody talking – even getting herself banned from MTV in America on a couple of occasions. However, despite the controversy – or perhaps because of it – when VH1 showed its 100 Greatest Videos programme in 2001, Madonna had more entries on the list than anyone else and two of her most controversial videos were in the top 10 – Justify My Love at number seven and *Like A Prayer* at number two, beaten only by Michael Jackson's *Thriller*.

Although it's easy to forget now, given all that Madonna has done since, the video for *Like A Prayer* caused a major scandal in its day. It all began with Madonna's $5 million advertising contract with Pepsi. She agreed that she would appear in one of their commercials, while benefiting from the advert's use of her single, *Like A Prayer*, before the record was released. Pepsi would benefit from having their product associated with the top female entertainer in the world.

Shown for the first time during the commercial break in *The Cosby Show* on 2 March 1989 – and at a similar time all around the globe – approximately

MISCHIEF

250 million people worldwide saw the two-minute advert. "The global media buy and unprecedented debut of this long-awaited single will put Pepsi first and foremost in the consumers' minds," bragged the Pepsi press release. The plan was to run a 30-second version of the advert during the summer months. However, the plans were to be changed when Madonna's own video for *Like A Prayer* was unveiled.

In what is now widely regarded as one of her best videos, *Like A Prayer* features Madonna with stigmata on her hands, dancing in front of burning crosses and embracing a black actor who can also be seen in the video portraying a Christ-like figure. There was an immediate backlash from religious groups and family organisations. Although this video had nothing to do with the Pepsi advertisement, many tarred the fizzy drink company with the same brush they were using to besmirch Madonna. Executive director of the American Family Association, Donald Wildmon, wrote an article in *USA Today*, which he concluded by saying: "For the next year, I will not drink Pepsi. If enough others join me, perhaps respect for religious beliefs of others will be helped tremendously. At least it is a start." This was not

MISCHIEF

the kind of publicity that Pepsi was looking for from its association with Madonna, and the deal was abandoned. Not that Madonna suffered. *Like a Prayer* went to number one and she even got to keep the $5 million fee from Pepsi.

The video for Madonna's 2001 single *What It Feels Like For a Girl* was banned by MTV America. The video was directed by her husband Guy Ritchie who had made his name directing the British gangster flicks *Lock, Stock and Two Smoking Barrels* and *Snatch* – both certified '18' by the British Board of Film Classification – it is perhaps not surprising that Ritchie chose violence as the theme for his wife's video.

What It Feels Like For a Girl features Madonna driving an old woman around a city and having various violent fantasies on the way – such as running over people in a car park, threatening policemen with water pistols, and relieving a man of his money. After abandoning one car and stealing another, she then drives the vehicle – still with the old lady and herself inside – into a concrete post, presumably killing them both.

Ironically, although American MTV banned the video saying it contained excessive violence, when *What It Feels Like For a Girl* was reviewed by the British Board of Film Classification for its release on DVD, they only gave it a '12' certificate. European MTV playlisted the video, but only for viewing after midnight. Madonna's fans argued that videos by other artists were more violent, and that Madonna was being judged too harshly because of her reputation for rocking the boat.

Two of the videos that helped her earn that reputation, *Justify My Love* and *Erotica*, upset many of those who regarded themselves as the moral majority. Both videos contained sensual, sexual images that proved too racy for MTV and its teenage audience. *Justify My Love* was banned outright from the channel, while *Erotica* was relegated to a late-night slot.

Sex and sexuality

SEX AND SEXUALITY

adonna has used sex and sexuality as a means of shocking her audiences for some time. Indeed early in her career, in 1985, nude photographs taken shortly after she'd arrived in New York surfaced in both *Playboy* and *Penthouse* magazines. Her public statement at the time was: "I'm not ashamed of anything". Like Marilyn Monroe before her, Madonna rode out any negative publicity – of which there was very little – by joking about it. During her performance at Live Aid she kept her coat on throughout her performance, despite the warm temperatures and bright stage lights. "I ain't taking s**t off today,"

SEX AND SEXUALITY

she shouted to her audience. "You might hold it against me in 10 years." Of course, by the time 10 years had passed the public had seen much, much more of Madonna.

The *Playboy* and *Penthouse* photographs hinted there was perhaps an exhibitionist side to Madonna. In 1992 any doubts that this was the case were dismissed with the publication of her book *Sex*. This 128-page volume was spiral bound with stainless steel covers and was wrapped in sealed in silver Mylar which meant that it would have to be purchased – at a cost of $49.95 – before a Madonna fan or voyeur could take a peek inside. But what a treat for them when they did!

Madonna's erotic fantasies were photographed by Steven Meisel in stunning black and white, and narrated by Madonna via a character called Dita whom she'd specially created for the book. This book was not available to anyone under the age of 18, and with good reason. Most of the pictures feature Madonna partially dressed, and a great many of them feature her completely nude. She is seen pictured alongside celebrities such as Naomi Campbell, Vanilla Ice and Isabella Rossellini. Although the pictures are definitely erotica rather than

SEX AND SEXUALITY

pornography, for some people, Madonna had crossed the line of decency.

Somewhat predictably, *Sex* whipped up quite a fuss in the press. Although Richard Harrington, from *The Washington Post*, kept a level head, writing: "Madonna [is] one of the few women or men with the nerve and savvy to publicly explore these particular territories. Maybe the only one... For her, sex is play and this is still her playground." Not all the articles about *Sex* were as balanced as this piece was, however.

Madonna was condemned by people who had not even seen a copy of the book. In later years, after she had become a mother and was widely regarded to have 'calmed down', Madonna spoke of the whole *Sex* phenomenon saying she had no regrets. The only problem she saw was that her album, *Erotica*, which was released at the same time was overlooked. She claimed: "Everything I did for the next three years was dwarfed by my book."

Among the projects 'dwarfed' by *Sex* was *Body of Evidence*, which also featured the Material Girl not wearing much of anything, frolicking in bed with Willem Dafoe. Once again the so-called 'moral majority' were quick to complain, but since they hadn't finished complaining about *Sex* yet, *Body of Evidence* got tied up in the furore, as did the *Erotica* album.

Even when she is being herself rather than putting on a performance, she frequently manages to cause controversy thanks to the sheer force of her personality and her outspokenness. This was particularly evident when she released the documentary *In Bed With Madonna*. For a woman who has been described as "an entertainer whose personality is an outrageous blend of Little Orphan Annie, Margaret Thatcher, and Mae West", the idea of her own documentary provided Madonna with the opportunity to let her public see her as she really was – or as she really wanted them to see her.

Nothing was off limits, she told Alek Kashishian and his team of cameramen as they joined her backstage on her 1991 Blonde Ambition World Tour. Although she later changed the rules slightly – banning the cameras from a business meeting and a reunion with her grandmother – essentially *In Bed With Madonna* shows the superstar laid bare (figuratively this time). Many sides to Madonna's personality were revealed through the film (which was called *Truth or Dare* when released in America).

MADONNA

SEX AND SEXUALITY

In one scene, Madonna's theory about all publicity being good publicity is spoken aloud after one of her dancer's voices concern about not getting any work after simulating sex on-stage. "In this country", the singer explains, "it works the other way round. The more notorious you are, the more you are going to work! Don't you guys understand that?"

When the tour hits Toronto, Canada, authorities inform her that if she does not remove the part of the show where she imitates masturbation during *Like a Virgin*, they will close the show and arrest the cast for public indecency. When Madonna finds out that she would probably be booked, fined and released, she decides the risk is worth it and continues with the show as planned. The authorities back down, but not before Madonna makes a big fuss over their warning, playing it up to the press and enjoying the attention that comes with being notorious. In her prayer before the Canada show, rather than asking God for a great show, she condemns "the fascist state of Toronto".

In Bed With Madonna showed her fans, and the world, that Madonna was an expert in making the most of her fame. She could be hard-nosed and cutting where necessary. Her business savvy surprised some people who had previously viewed her as the Boy Toy she pretended to be in the mid-Eighties, and she gained new respect from a wider audience.

However, the documentary also showed the less brash side of Madonna. It showed her visiting her mother's grave and worrying about "toning down" her show for her father when he came to watch. It was the inclusion of moments such as these that made Madonna's then boyfriend Warren Beatty say: "She doesn't want to live off-camera. Why would you bother to say something if it's off-camera?" Tellingly, this comment is left in the film. She does not, however, allow cameras into a business meeting. It is okay for the public to see Madonna the superstar, but they are not allowed to see Madonna the business woman. The important point is that Madonna remains in control of what we can and cannot see throughout the documentary.

She later said of the film to *Vanity Fair*: "People will say, 'She knows the camera is on, she's just acting' ... You could watch it and say, 'I still don't know Madonna', and good. Because you will never know the real me. Ever." Indeed, it is Madonna's skill at protecting her true personality

SEX AND SEXUALITY

that enables her to change her style and image so frequently and so successfully.

One of the strangest claims Madonna has had to contend with is that she is an anti-feminist. This label was first applied to her during the Boy Toy years, and seemed to stick for a while afterwards. Madonna refuted the claims as "ludicrous", explaining that women can be powerful and respected regardless of how they dress.

When Britney Spears was asked about Madonna for a 2001, BBC documentary, she supported the view that Madonna demonstrates that you can be feminine and still be a feminist icon. Spears said of her idol: "She's very independent and doesn't care what other people think. That's very empowering for teenagers and for women in general. She has amazing drive and ambition when she's on-stage. You can't help but watch and admire her."

Madonna's recent return to her shocking ways – kissing Spears and Christina Aguilera at the MTV Video Music Awards – showed her ability to capture front page headlines remains undiminished, despite the fact she is over 40 and is married with two children. Not only has the Material Girl turned Maternal Girl aged remarkably well, but

SEX AND SEXUALITY

she has lost none of her ability to capture attention with the passing years and increased responsibilities.

When she hit 40 in 1998, she spoke to Jonathan Ross about her age. "Not only do we suffer from racism and sexism," she ranted, "but we also suffer from ageism. Once you reach a certain age you're not allowed to be adventurous, you're not allowed to be sexual, I mean is there a rule? Are you supposed to just die when you're 40?"

Indeed, if anyone has proved that a powerful personality can transcend the ageing process then it's Madonna. Never afraid to speak her mind – or if the mood takes her, to shed her clothes – the superstar has successfully kept herself in the public eye for nearly 20 years, doing what she does best while at the same time doing what nobody else could get away with. As she said to CW Arrington, from *Time* magazine: "I present my view on life in my work. The provocation slaps you in the face, and the ambiguity makes you say, well, is it that or is it that? You are forced to have a discussion about it in your mind."

Madonna has an amazing ability to make people think and to get people talking. And, where necessary, to cause a commotion.

Men

MADONNA

MEN

abelling herself a Boy Toy in the Eighties brought Madonna a great deal of publicity, as well as some criticism from women who felt that she was an anti-feminist. However, as the superstar has proved time and time again, Madonna is a feminine feminist — someone who does not try to hide her femininity, yet expects to be taken as seriously as a man. She is a role model for many modern women.

So what role do men play in the feminine feminist equation? It is interesting to note that, despite her reputation as a strong woman with a dominant personality, the men who have figured

MEN

most prominently in Madonna's love life have all had strong personalities themselves – no hen-pecked husbands for the twice-married performer. Indeed both of her spouses have been stars in their own right outside the relationship, so there was never any risk of them becoming Mr Madonna (although it could be argued that this is a fate that befell some of her lesser-known romancers).

What follows is not a comprehensive list of all the men who have ever been involved with Madonna, nor are we concerning ourselves with tabloid tales or gossip column headlines. While recalling some of the briefer encounters in Madonna's life, this is primarily a look at the three main relationships of Madonna's life – those with Sean Penn, Carlos Leon and Guy Ritchie.

Having arrived in New York in the Seventies, her early relationships were often with men on the outskirts of the music business – such as Dan Gilroy, Steve Bray and John 'Jellybean' Benitez. Another early relationship from the New York years was with artist Jean-Michel Basquiat. An extremely talented but sadly ultimately self-destructive man, Basquiat died from a heroin overdose in 1988, at the age of 27.

After her star began to shine, journalists

MEN

started asking the controversial singer what she thought about the more conventional practices of settling down and raising a family. Rather than dismiss the idea out of hand – as many must have expected her to do – Madonna stated in May 1985 that she would like to get married one day and have children. She did not have to wait long on the first count, although the patter of tiny feet would be another decade in arriving.

Madonna's 1985 wedding to Sean Penn was one of the celebrity events of the year, with a guest list that featured the cream of Hollywood – including Tom Cruise, Martin Sheen, Carrie Fisher and Cher – as well as Madonna's friends from her time in New York and family members (Madonna's sister Paula was maid of honour). The wedding took place on 16 August – Madonna's 27th birthday, Penn would turn 25 the day after.

Madonna wore a $10,000 strapless white gown with a 10-foot long train designed by Marlene Stewart, while the groom was movie-star-handsome in a double-breasted Gianni Versace suit. The location – the million-dollar beachside home of a real estate developer friend of Penn's – had been a closely guarded secret due to the level of press attention directed towards the couple, not to mention the famous guests. Invitations did not have the location printed on them, and guests were informed where to go by a phone call on the day of the wedding itself.

Sadly, despite this, the press discovered where the ceremony was being held and bombarded the location, flying so close in their helicopters that the breeze they created knocked guests' hats off. Penn did not take well to this invasion of his privacy, scrawling a warning in 20-feet letters in the sand and discharging a firearm into the air. Despite the sound of helicopters buzzing overhead, the service continued and later Penn toasted his new wife, "the most beautiful woman in the world", on the balcony. Madonna's father, Tony, gave her away.

While not as famous as his wife, Penn's career as a film actor was going well in 1985. Seen as something of a 'bad boy' actor in the press, he was a member of the infamous Brat Pack, after appearing in the 1982 film *Fast Times at Ridgemont High* alongside Jennifer Jason Leigh and Phoebe Cates.

Although Madonna was an actress as well as a singer, following the poor response at the box office of *Shanghai Surprise* – the film the couple appeared in together – Madonna and Penn decided

MEN

to keep their careers separate. Madonna admitted that although they had decided not to work together, Penn was still a source of creative inspiration, most notably in the case of her 1986 album *True Blue*. Holden wrote in his article: *"True Blue* takes its title from a favourite expression of Sean Penn, and is a tribute, according to Madonna, 'to my husband's very pure vision of love.'"

Sadly this union was not to last. Before long the strength of both Madonna and Penn's personalities seemed incompatible. Not that they didn't try to keep the marriage on track. Despite filing for divorce in 1987, Madonna decided to give the relationship another go, but it only lasted until late 1988, with divorce following in 1989. Penn diplomatically summed up the problem in their relationship by saying that they were "reading from different scripts".

Since the end of his marriage to Madonna, Penn has gone on to father two children with Robin Wright, whom he married in 1996. He has enjoyed box office success and critical acclaim as an actor, earning Oscar nominations for *Dead Man Walking*, *Sweet and Lowdown* and *I Am Sam*. He finally won the Academy Award in 2004 for his role as Jimmy Markum in *Mystic River*.

MEN

After her first marriage ended, Madonna was the subject of many rumours which linked her with a series of different men and one woman – her friend Sandra Bernhard. One of the rumours linked the Material Girl to John F Kennedy Jr. Madonna had always been outspoken about her love of Marilyn Monroe, who had famously had an affair with JFK, commentators were quick to ask whether history was repeating itself.

Madonna was certainly a fan of both John F Kennedy Jr and his mother Jackie Kennedy Onassis. This was evident in a 1996 interview she gave shortly after the birth of her daughter. "I would like her to have as normal a life as possible," she said of Lourdes. Adding: "Look at John Kennedy Jr. He's been photographed since he was two and he turned out okay. He had a very strong, intelligent mother." Sadly, just like his father before him, John F Kennedy suffered a tragically early death. He died in a plane crash near Martha's Vineyard in July 1999, at the age of 38, with his wife Carolyn and her sister Lauren Bessette.

One of Madonna's brief encounters that so delighted the press took place in 1990. While working together on the movie *Dick Tracy*, Madonna began seeing movie-legend Warren Beatty who was over 20 years her senior. Despite cynics in the press labelling the relationship a publicity stunt, the pair seemed genuinely taken with each other. Towards the end of the relationship, Beatty was featured in *In Bed With Madonna*, where he looked uncomfortable and made his now infamous remarks about his girlfriend's unwillingness to live off-camera.

Other romances in the early Nineties were with model Tony Ward – who appeared in her videos for *Cherish* and *Justify My Love*, as well as in her book *Sex* – and basketball star Dennis Rodman. With a reputation almost as outrageous as Madonna's, Rodman disappointed the singer when he revealed intimate details of their affair in his biography *Bad As I Wanna Be*. Madonna dismissed Rodman by saying his information was "untrue" and that the only reason his book sold well was because he had spoken about their sex life.

Vanilla Ice, a rap star whose real name was Robert Van Winkle, also had a brief liaison with Madonna, and appeared with her on the pages of her *Sex* book. Ten years younger than Madonna, Vanilla Ice had a big success in 1990 with his number one single *Ice Ice Baby*, however, his career was on a downward turn by the time *Sex* was published in 1992.

One man Madonna never had her way with was Spanish heartthrob Antonio Banderas. Despite calling him "very sexy" in her *In Bed With Madonna* documentary, she claimed that she was not embarrassed when they ended up working together on *Evita* some years later. By the time they filmed *Evita*, Banderas was separated from his first wife Ana Leza, but heavily involved with the woman who was to become his second wife, Melanie Griffith. Madonna said that she and Banderas got together and laughed about the whole *In Bed With Madonna* business.

Madonna herself was romantically involved with someone during the making of *Evita*. Although he was neither a celebrity boyfriend nor a future husband, Carlos Leon was certainly one of Madonna's most significant relationships.

She first spotted him in September 1994 when he cycled past her while she was jogging in Central Park. They checked each other out and, although it is hard to imagine a superstar approaching someone she's never met, Madonna did just that and began a conversation with Leon. He was a personal trainer with dark

MEN

Latino good looks and dreams of making the Olympic cycling team. Shortly after their first meeting, they began dating.

Leon and Madonna planned to start a family together after Madonna had finished filming *Evita*, so it must have been quite a surprise when during production she discovered she was pregnant. Although both prospective parents were over the moon with the news, when Madonna was asked if she and Leon planned on marrying, she claimed there was no need.

When Madonna's pregnancy was announced to the media they began prying into Leon's background, which must have been very difficult for someone unused to life in the celebrity spotlight. He developed a distrust of the press who treated him like the superstar's stud service.

In the end, despite the birth of Lourdes on 14 October 1996, Madonna and Leon could not make their relationship work. Despite many offers to "tell all" about his time with the star, Leon has remained loyal to Madonna, proving himself to be one of the good guys in her life. He still sees his daughter Lourdes. These days he's an actor, enjoying a regular role as Carlos Martinez in the US prison drama *Oz* as well as other television and film roles.

After her split from Leon, Madonna dated Englishman Andy Bird, an actor and scriptwriter. Once again the press made a fuss about Madonna dating someone who did not occupy the same celebrity world as she does. This time Madonna got angry, speaking out in *Vogue* magazine. "Why does the man have to be the one who makes more money?" she asked. "It's pathetic and sexist and disgusting, and if people don't change the way they view this thing – the man and woman's place in society – nothing's ever going to change."

Although Madonna's relationship with UK-based Bird was not long-lived, England was the setting for a meeting that would change her life. At a party held by Sting's wife Trudi Styler in the summer of 1998 Madonna met the film-maker and director Guy Ritchie, who later admitted that meeting the superstar was the only reason he went to the party.

Although much of the talk at the party was business talk – Sting had recently appeared in Ritchie's gangster film *Lock, Stock and Two Smoking Barrels*, and Ritchie and partner Matthew Vaughn were wondering whether Madonna's company Maverick would be interested

MEN

in putting out the soundtrack, which it did – Ritchie certainly made a good impression on Madonna. She later remembered in an interview with *The Face* magazine: "I had a whole premonition of my life fast-forward. My head didn't just turn, my head spun round on my body. I was taken by his confidence."

Born in 1968 – making him 10 years Madonna's junior – Ritchie's parents John and Amber divorced when he was young, his mother went on to marry Sir Michael Leighton on whose estate the young Guy Ritchie learnt to shoot and fish. This life of respectability in the English countryside was something Ritchie would first rebel against and then return to, accompanied the second time around by Madonna an all-American girl who found she could effortlessly transform into the role of English country lady.

Ritchie's films although nowhere near Madonna's levels of success, are nevertheless doing very well. *Lock, Stock...* made £18 million in the UK (having only cost £1 million), and was publicly supported by Tom Cruise when it was released in America. Then for the follow-up, *Snatch*, Brad Pitt accepted just 10 per cent of his standard fee to appear as an incoherent boxer.

MEN

So Ritchie, with his dirty blonde hair and quick grin, won Madonna's heart and they embarked on a relationship. Madonna said that he treated her "like a normal person, not an icon" and she began to act that way as well, accompanying Ritchie to pubs where she chatted with the rather astounded locals. The superstar, who Ritchie calls 'Madge' or 'the missus', even moved to London.

Madonna and Ritchie seemed so happy together that it came as no surprise when they announced in February 2000: "We're happy to confirm rumours that we're expecting a child at the end of the year." Although Rocco did not wait that long to be born, entering the world earlier than expected on 11 August.

When Madonna brought Rocco home she was about to feed him when she noticed a crumpled paper bag at the side of the bed. She was about to put it in the bin when she noticed that there was something inside it. It was a diamond ring accompanied by a note. Guy Ritchie was going to make an honest woman of Madonna.

Now there was another wedding to plan, location was all important – especially as Madonna wanted to avoid a repeat of the press intrusion that had nearly ruined her ceremony

MEN

with Sean Penn. Ex-footballer and now film actor Vinnie Jones is said to have recommended Skibo Castle in the Scottish Highlands. This exclusive venue is well-known for its discretion, and has attracted such stars as Jack Nicholson and Michael Douglas. Plans were also made to baptise Rocco at the nearby Dornoch Cathedral.

All 51 bedrooms at Skibo Castle – once the home of steel and railway magnate Andrew Carnegie – were booked for the wedding party and guests. All those attending the ceremony, including staff, had to remain on the property for the five days leading up to the wedding ceremony, except for when they attended Rocco's baptism. This would not have been a hardship, though, as Skibo Castle is the epitome of luxurious living, set in 7,500 acres of beautiful Scottish countryside.

Rocco was baptised on 21 December 2000, and some beautiful pictures were taken of him with his famous mother and father on the steps of Dornoch Cathedral. These were the only pictures the press were going to get of Madonna and Ritchie on their trip to Scotland, despite booking out hotels and trying to get into the castle, all attempts to get pictures of the wedding failed. To this day, no photograph of Madonna on her second wedding day has appeared in the press and no official photograph was ever released, although Jean Baptiste Mondino documented the whole thing as official photographer. Mondino was the director responsible for Madonna's videos for *Don't Tell Me*, *Love Don't Live Here Anymore*, *Human Nature*, *Open Your Heart* and the controversial *Justify My Love*.

Remarkably, not one guest sold their story to the press, so there has been no first-hand exposé of the day's events. All in all, Madonna won her battle against press intrusion.

What we do know about the ceremony is that it took place on 22 December. The bride wore a dress designed by close friend Stella McCartney and rumours abounded that either McCartney or Gwyneth Paltrow was Madonna's maid of honour. The groom wore a kilt of Hunting Mackintosh tartan in what is thought to be a tribute to his grandfather, war hero Major Stewart Ritchie, who served with the Seaforth Highlanders.

The ceremony was conducted by Rev Susan Brown, who had also baptised Rocco and famous guests to both celebrations included McCartney, Paltrow, Rupert Everett, Sting and Trudi Styler.

Later Madonna spoke about the wedding.

MEN

She said: "It was truly a magical religious experience... It was very personal and very intimate. We could both really look around and feel that everybody was rooting for us and supporting us."

Motherhood

MADONNA

n Monday 15 September 2003, a children's book entitled *The English Roses* went on sale in the UK. The day before, its author held a launch party in Kensington where she read extracts from the book to the children and celebrities present. The press attending the event fired questions at the author, which she answered patiently and politely.

"I like little kids better than big people," she said with a smile. "They don't have any bad habits yet. At least, not permanent ones."

Although this was not Madonna as most of her fans were used to seeing her, they packed out the

MOTHERHOOD

event anyway. This was the new Madonna – Maternal Girl rather than Material Girl – the author of something that her children, and many other children around the world can enjoy. Not that this means that she is respectably dull, the new Madonna is still not adverse to shaking up the public's perception of her. It is a tribute to Madonna's wide-ranging talent that she can jump from Maternal Girl to Shock-Factor Queen, and then jump right back again. However, there can be no doubt that motherhood – above everything else in her life – has made Madonna complete and happy.

Back in 1985, just three months before marrying Sean Penn, Madonna said: "I do want to get married and have kids. I don't know when, but... I would definitely like to have a child." Despite this statement, it took more than a decade before Madonna started a family, doing her bit to show that a modern woman really can have it all – a successful and fulfiling 20-year career, a family, and a new start in a whole new country.

The switch from Material to Maternal began in 1996, during the making of *Evita*. Madonna discovered she was pregnant before filming finished, which created something of an onset panic as the director and producers frantically

MOTHERHOOD

worked out how long they had before the superstar's bump would start ruining the line of her costumes. Nausea in the dusty heat of Argentina was another problem that the ever-professional performer had to deal with.

During the filming of *Evita*, Madonna kept a diary for publication in *Vanity Fair* magazine. Towards the end of production she wrote: "The intensity of the scenes we've been shooting and the amount of emotional work and concentration needed to get through the day are so mentally and physically exhausting that I'm sure I will need to be institutionalised when it is over."

However, all the hard work she put into *Evita* paid off, the film was a smash hit, and as soon as production ended, Madonna was free to fully experience her pregnancy and spend time with the father of her child, Carlos Leon. By her own admission Madonna enjoyed being pregnant, she did not have to endure severe morning sickness or any unusual cravings while she was pregnant with her first child. She said afterwards that she was comfortable most of the time and enjoyed being able to eat what she wanted after years of exercising and watching her figure. The only time she felt uncomfortable, she said, was in the last few weeks.

MADONNA

MOTHERHOOD

With her pregnancy scrutinised by the world's press, there was media speculation over such issues as whether Madonna and Leon would marry, indeed whether they should marry, and whether or not Madonna would make a good mother. This continual commentary angered the star, who spoke out: "Everything I do is scrutinised so I shouldn't be surprised that it continued when I was pregnant. I try to have a sense of humour about it but it does irritate me... My having a child is not for public consumption. It's not a career move. It's not a performance to be judged and rated. Nor is my role as a mother."

After an uncomfortable last couple of weeks, Madonna's daughter – Lourdes Maria Ciccone Leon – was born on 14 October 1996 at the Good Samaritan Hospital in Los Angeles. After 16 hours of labour ending in a Caesarean section, the new arrival was named after a town in France associated with miracles, and weighed in at 6 pounds and 9 ounces.

For the first month of Lourdes' life, all Madonna did was care for her daughter and receive visits from family members and friends, all eager to see the dark-haired child who looked so like her mother at that same age. Slowly Madonna

MOTHERHOOD

started sitting at her desk and working again, but she was hazy when asked about her career plans, saying that she wanted to spend less time working and more time with her daughter.

By December 1996 Madonna impressed all those at the premiere for *Evita* with her newly svelte figure. Her date for the premiere was Leon. Although her relationship with him was not to last, Lourdes – known within the family as Lola – still sees her father regularly.

It was with the imminent arrival of Lourdes that Madonna began to embrace Kabbalah - the mystical Jewish teachings made popular by Rabbi Philip Berg. Madonna discovered the faith during her pregnancy and went about studying it in Los Angeles with Rabbi Eitan Yardeni. Disciples of Kabbalah – including Elizabeth Taylor, Barbra Streisand, Naomi Campbell, Mick Jagger and Jerry Hall. Those that believe wear a thin red bracelet to protect them from the evil eye, as well as reinforcing their belief in the principles of friendship, spirituality and knowledge. It was reported that Madonna also donated funds for a new building in London for the Kabbalah Centre.

Madonna used the teachings of Kabbalah as the inspiration behind her children's stories. She has frequently spoken of her desire to raise her children with the wisdom of many religions, rather than follow the strict Catholic upbringing she experienced. Although she did baptise both her children in the Catholic faith, it is fair to say their lives are more influenced by the Kabbalah teachings.

Madonna's next album after Lourdes' arrival also presented the former Madonna's more spiritual side to her fans. *Ray of Light*'s credit notes reflect that Kabbalah was a major influence during the making of the album, which featured songs about her new daughter as well as reflections on the problems of celebrity and Madonna's memories of her own mother.

When reviewing *Ray of Light*, Joan Anderman of the *Boston Globe*, wrote: "Motherhood has been known to soften the hardest hearts; in Madonna's case it seems to have torn open a window-size hole." He went on to praise the album claiming it aspired to something deeper that a simple dance record.

If motherhood had softened Madonna career-wise, she was not going easy on her small daughter. Although opting against a traditional strict Catholic upbringing she still tried to raise her daughter in a similar way to how she herself had been raised by her father. Her friend, film

MOTHERHOOD

star and TV presenter Rosie O'Donnell has said of Madonna: "She's a tough-love kind of mother. For instance, she doesn't want her child watching TV... And no junk food for Lourdes either." Indeed Madonna, who was also not allowed to watch television as a child, has spoken out about protecting her children from watching violent and sexual images on TV. However, "tough-love" or not, there can be no doubt that Madonna is a kind and caring mother to little Lourdes.

Although she was 38 when she gave birth for the first time, Madonna was determined that she would have another child, but that she would wait until she was in a secure relationship before this happened. This relationship came when she met British film-maker Guy Ritchie, and they announced Madonna's pregnancy in March 2000 with a statement that ended by saying: "We would be grateful if the media would kindly allow us some privacy at this special time and we thank you all for your good wishes."

Privacy was perhaps too much to hope for, but the couple dealt with the attention well, although the constant questioning must have been doubly exhausting for a woman in Madonna's condition. In April the couple spoke out to deny

MOTHERHOOD

rumours that they knew the sex of the baby. In June Madonna appeared at the Leicester Square Odeon for the premiere of her film *The Next Best Thing*. Dressed in a long black dress and frock coat, Madonna's baby bump was on display for all to see as she told the assembled media of her strange cravings for eggs and olives.

Although not expected to give birth until September, Madonna went into labour early and had her baby on 11 August 2000 at Cedars-Sinai Hospital in Los Angeles, just hours after calling British hospitals "old and Victorian". This time the baby was a boy, weighing in at 5 pounds and 9 ounces. The proud parents decided to call their new son Rocco John Ritchie. As is common with premature babies, Rocco suffered from jaundice at first, and was kept in intensive care for five days as his lungs were not yet fully developed.

Rumours about Rocco's health filled the newspapers, until both Madonna's spokesperson and then Ritchie himself spoke out to put matters to right. Spokeswoman Liz Rosenberg said: "Madonna and the baby and her daughter, Lourdes, are all home, happy, healthy and thriving," while Ritchie was every inch the proud father, saying: "Everything is fine since she came out of hospital. I am extremely happy to be a father and I am extremely happy that the pair of them are in the condition that they are in."

So with family complete, Madonna and Ritchie set about raising their children as normally as was possible for a couple in such a position of celebrity. This was never going to be an easy task. A poll in *Star* magazine to find Britain's most eligible bachelors in October 2000 featured Rocco at number 20, even though he was less than three months old at the time. Both of Madonna's children also have websites devoted to them, as well as photographers and reporters following them around.

Despite her mother's fame, and the fame of many of her mother's friends, Lourdes still gets star struck, such as when she met pop princess Britney Spears and had to hide behind her nanny's skirt. Spears later explained: "Her nanny said that she normally talks a lot, but she was being really quiet and shy. She looked at her nanny and said, 'Tell her, will you? Just tell her that I have all the watches and all of her Barbies and stuff'. I thought it was so sweet." By all accounts, Madonna's two children are growing up refreshingly unaffected. Pictures have appeared showing the whole family washing the car together, Lourdes pushing Rocco in his buggy and of Ritchie and his son playing together in the park.

Madonna is now also a self-confessed Anglophile, having moved to England during the early days of her relationship with Ritchie. While she was pregnant with Rocco she said of her new surroundings: "It's interesting, because one always thinks about England as being this repressed, tradition-based place, where everyone has this uptight prim way of relating to each other. But, in fact, Americans, who are known for being boisterous and straightforward, are puritanical, so it's a strange paradox. Because on the outside it seems like everyone in England is uptight, but actually they're not." She went on to comment that she couldn't get used to seeing naked Page Three girls in the newspapers. A humourous observation and more than a little surprising coming from the woman who posed completely nude for a book about her own sexual fantasies.

We know everything (or at least we think we know everything) about 'Madge' now she is here in the UK. Celebrity magazines tell us that she gets her hair highlighted at Daniel Galvin and that she drinks in The Sanderson and eats at San Lorenzo. She led the way and Gwyneth Paltrow has

MOTHERHOOD

followed, both Americans taking delight in starting anew in Great Britain. Author J Randy Taraborrelli, who has written a biography of Madonna, commented about the singer in a BBC documentary: "I have noticed recently there is a love affair with her going on in Britain. It is like this wonderful and long extended honeymoon where there seems to be a sense of dignity around the way she is pursued."

However dignified they are being, the attention from the UK's infamous tabloid press and celebrity-obsessed media can still get too much for our favourite import. Madonna recently took a UK magazine to task when it suggested that she was expecting again – a presumption based on the evidence that (a) the star had dyed her hair brown and (b) she was wearing baggy clothes. Her spokeswoman, Liz Rosenberg, said at the time: "It's not true, it's not accurate. She dyed her hair brown instead of blonde – that does not confirm someone's pregnant." It certainly does not, but what this whole incident does confirm is that Madonna's life is as newsworthy to the media now as it ever was - despite claims of her "settling down" she remains fascinating for press and public alike.

MOTHERHOOD

And she also remains as successful. Her first children's book, *The English Roses*, is on sale in 100 countries, translated into 30 languages, and has so far sold more than 500,000 copies. A number of celebrities attended the London launch in September 2003, including Stella McCartney, Linda Barker and Patsy Palmer.

At the launch Madonna explained that she wrote *The English Roses* because, "I wanted to do something for my children... It is a story about learning to appreciate what we have ourselves and not to be fixated on what other people have." The central character Binah is based on Lourdes, and her struggle to fit in. "In school often children can be quite mean and ostracise her because I'm her mother," Madonna said. "Everyone thinks, 'She's got everything so we won't pay attention to her.'"

In Madonna's prepared statement, issued to the press at the time of the book's release, she said: "The idea first came about through my Kabbalah teacher, who suggested that I share the spiritual wisdom I've learned studying the Kabbalah by writing children's stories.

"And then there's my own children. Raising kids makes most people, including myself, grow up at least a little. It also makes us more responsible

MOTHERHOOD

and more thoughtful about our own actions and their consequences for those around us... I hope these children's books inspire kids of all ages – even grown-up ones."

The English Roses was the first of five 'morality tales'. The second, *Mr Peabody's Apples* – concerning a teacher falsely accused of theft, was released in November 2003, while *Yakov and the Seven Thieves* will follow late in 2004.

Madonna's ability to shock has certainly not dimmed with the arrival of motherhood. Indeed, her *What It Feels Like For a Girl* video, the Britney Spears/Christina Aguilera kiss plus her Reinvention and Drowned World Tours have all happened since Madonna became a mother. What seems to have changed is Madonna's attitude to shocking the press and public. Before Lourdes' birth, Madonna was seen as the ultimate career woman with the ultimate career – author, model, singer, actress, nothing got in the way of her success. When her daughter arrived, Madonna appeared to need less press attention and seemed more settled.

When she got together with Guy Ritchie, moved to England and gave birth to Rocco, she was almost completely transformed from the woman that she had been a decade before... or was she? The Madonna of 1985 had wanted marriage, children and a career too – everything the Madonna of today has.

In 2003 the superstar told Jo Whiley on Radio 1 that she felt there were too few inspirational female role models in music. "Women that I really looked up to when I was first starting out were Debbie Harry and Chrissie Hynde," she said. "I thought they were really strong. I loved their sense of irony which I think is missing from pop music right now."

Whether Madonna realises it or not, she is an inspiration role model herself, not just for young performers and the new fans who are drawn to her music, but for those who have grown up with her music, and those who are settling down with her.

12

Megastar

MADONNA

MEGASTAR

So who is Madonna? Is she the caring wife and mother or the woman who recently posed for a photo wearing a Marie-Antoinette-style wig and with the camera positioned so that the casual observer couldn't help peering down her cleavage? Is she the woman who wrote about her sensual fantasies for the controversial tome *Sex* or the author who tackled jealousy and bullying in her children's book *The English Roses*? Is she an Anglophile or an all-American girl?

Madonna proves that it is possible to be all of these things. She has reinvented her image countless times, yet never appears to be anything other than herself. Her every image becomes iconic, and there have been impersonators at each stage of her career, from the Boy Toy years, past the days where she appeared wearing a Jean Paul Gaultier-designed conical bustier, through to the cowboy chic of *Don't Tell Me*. And, speaking of imitators, Madonna also holds the honour of being the most performed artist on ITV's *Stars in Their Eyes*, with eight wannabes attempting to copy her across the first 14 series.

She has had number one singles in the UK in the Eighties, Nineties and Noughties, and, with the exception of 1988, she has so far enjoyed a UK top 10 hit every year since 1984. All but three of her singles have reached the top 10 in the Billboard Dance/Club Play chart in America. She has an entry in the *Guinness Book of World Records* as the person to go through the highest number of costume changes in a movie. In *Evita* she wore 85 costumes, including 39 hats, 45 pairs of shoes and 56 pairs of earrings.

She has won almost every award going, including Grammys, MTV Video Music Awards, American Music Awards, Brit Awards, Blockbuster Entertainment Awards and Golden Globes. In 2003 she won the American Music

MEGASTAR

Awards' Michael Jackson International Artist of the Year Award.

In short, Madonna is a legend in her own lifetime. Not only a singer, she is also a talented actress who has appeared in Oscar-nominated movies and is the proud recipient of a much-coveted Golden Globe (for her performance in *Evita*). Not only that, but she has appeared on both West End and Broadway stages, as well as producing films through her own company. Her appearance in the London stage show *Up For Grabs* won her the Theatre Event Of The Year award, at the Whatsonstage.com Theatregoers Choice Awards.

She has been a runway model for Jean-Paul Gaultier, who say he is fascinated by the way she dresses. However well-dressed she may have been, when she appeared on the catwalk for him, Gaultier famously featured Madonna bare-breasted. He also designed the costumes for Madonna's Blonde Ambition tour. "That was one of the best times of my career," Gaultier said some years later.

In 1998 she won three VH1 Fashion Awards, for Most Stylish Artist, The Versace Award and Most Fashionable Artist and in 1991 she was named by *People* magazine as one of the 50 most beautiful people in the world. In 1993 German *Elle* named her The Greatest Fashion Trendsetter of the World.

It could be argued that Madonna has also conquered the difficult to control internet. In October 2000 she won her battle with a cybersquatter who was using the domain name madonna.com to host a pornographic website. The following month the singer held a concert at Brixton Academy which was watched live on the internet by a record-breaking nine million people.

All this from a woman whose heart was broken at the age of five when her beloved mother died of breast cancer. And although they have had their differences through the years, her father's strong influence is clear to see as we watch Madonna raise her own children.

A global superstar, known the world over by her first name alone, Madonna has certainly come a long way from the days when she was the high school cheerleader who took the lead role in a production of *My Fair Lady*. She is also proud of the fact that she remains as ambitious as she ever was, claiming to feel the same "hunger" today as she did when she first left home.

It was this ambition that got Madonna to university, and that gave her the courage to leave that same institution against her father's wishes, halfway through her dance course, and head to New York. She had many friends and mentors back home like dance instructor Christopher Flynn, but all Madonna had when she arrived in the Big Apple were her dreams, her talent and her determination to succeed. It's a tribute to her talent that the woman who arrived in the big city with just a handful of dollars is now one of the richest women on the planet – with wealth often estimated at anything between $300 million and $600 million.

Although, career-wise, her love of dance gave way to music, Madonna never truly stopped dancing, and along the way made some of the best videos and danced on tour in front of sell-out, record-breaking crowds. Her dance chart success is unparalleled, and her hit *Vogue* introduced a new craze to dancefloors all over the world.

"I'm tough, ambitious and I know exactly what I want," Madonna once said. "If that makes me a bitch, OK." In a world that has often not known how to deal with powerful women, Madonna broke the mould sometimes dressed in a power suit and sometimes appearing feminine and coquettish, confusing those who thought they had her figured out. Madonna has retained control over her own career and image since the beginning, making her an inspiration to a generation of women.

When BBC1 made a documentary about her in 2001, the stars lined up to pay tribute to her. Britney Spears said: "I have been a huge fan of Madonna since I was a little girl. She's the first person that I've really looked up to." Kylie Minogue recognised Madonna's far-reaching appeal, saying: "People that don't know anything about pop music still know of Madonna. Her reach is way beyond pop music. Her ability to move with the times and the strength of her convictions is something unusual in pop music, where things are usually so transient."

Madonna's acceptance of alternate lifestyles has earned her a strong gay following. In fact she once described herself as "a gay man trapped inside a woman's body". Early trips to gay nightclubs with her mentor Christopher Flynn inspired her passion for the camp and the kitsch, and she was supportive of the fight against Aids even before she lost Flynn and several of her other close friends to the disease.

Sheer determination got Madonna her record contract, hard work and talent earned her that first hit single. However, at the beginning of Madonna's career, critics labelled her a one-hit wonder. Then that hit stretched to an album, and then another. Madonna is now the top-selling female artist in the world and those early critics have been forced to eat their words many times over.

While her use of religious imagery has often caused controversy, Madonna has never entirely broken free of the Catholic faith she was brought up with. Although she now follows the teachings of Kabbalah, she has had her children baptised and has admitted that Catholicism will always be a part of her life. During her most shocking years Madonna was quite forceful in her language and attitude, famously saying the f-word 13 times during a 1994 live interview with David Letterman. In recent years, however, she seems to have mellowed, taking up yoga and releasing music inspired by her spirituality rather than music in which the shock factor is paramount.

Although the public don't see Madonna the businesswoman, she is clearly a boardroom force to be reckoned with. Her company Maverick – in which Madonna holds a stake in with partners Guy Oseary and Ronnie Dashev – not only represents Alanis Morrisette and Madonna herself, but has also released soundtracks to such hit movies as *Kill Bill*,

50 First Dates and *Matrix Revolutions*.

Madonna's music videos have played a huge part in building up her image and fame throughout the years, and from the controversial to the comfortable, they are always fresh and different. When *Rolling Stone* magazine listed the Top 100 Music Videos Of All Time in 1993, Madonna had six videos on the list, more than any other artist. *Express Yourself* made the top ten, while the other entries were *Like a Prayer*, *Borderline*, *Vogue*, *Justify My Love* and *Oh Father*. VH1's 100 Greatest Videos programme also had a similarly successful result for Madonna.

Some would even go as far as calling Madonna's videos art, and a few of them have indeed been shown in museums such as the Pompidou Centre in Paris. Camille Paglia wrote of the *Justify My Love* video in 1992: "*Justify My Love* is truly avant-garde, at a time when that word has lost meaning in the flabby art world. It represents European sexuality of a kind we have not seen since the great foreign films of the Fifties and Sixties."

Madonna has always had a keen interest in art and in particular the artist Frida Kahlo.

Although the movie, 2002's *Frida*, was eventually made with Salma Hayek, Madonna's interest in the tragic Mexican artist Kahlo is something that many of her audience do not know about her. "I worship Frida Kahlo paintings," she told *Grammy* magazine, "because they reek of her sadness and pain."

Indeed, when Madonna loaned a Kahlo painting called *Self Portrait With Monkey* to the Tate Modern for their Surrealism display in October 2001, she said that it was "like letting go of one of my precious children. But I know she will be in good hands and the exhibit would not be complete without her". The star also uses Kahlo's painting called My Birth as a friendship test. If visitors do not like it, then Madonna does not like them.

Madonna is also a fan of the work and style of Art Deco erotic artists Tamara de Lempicka, and presented the Turner Prize to Martin Creed in 2001 – getting Channel 4, which was covering the event, in trouble when she swore, live on air, before the nine o'clock watershed.

In April 2003 an exhibition at the Deitch Gallery in New York called *X-STaTIC PRo=CeSS* caused some fuss when the three video and two photographic installations showed Madonna on a strip pole and spread, with arms and legs akimbo, on a table top. The photographer, Steven Klein, had also done adverts for Gucci, Versace and Calvin Klein. So not only is Madonna an art collector and creator of art with her videos, but she has actually become art herself.

In her movie career Madonna has had to fight the prejudice of the press every step of the way, as many other singers-turned-actresses have had to do. Despite losing some of the battles, she won the war with her award-winning role in *Evita*. Over the years she's also appeared as special guest on TV shows such as *Saturday Night Live* and *Will and Grace*. She admitted that she found her appearance on *Will and Grace* unnerving. "I wasn't nervous about the live audience, I think I got that covered," she said. "But what I was nervous about was, we'd rehearse, we'd rehearse, we'd rehearse and I finally had everything memorised. Then they'd come out with these really long things and I'd just think, 'I'm never going to remember that'.

"Somehow miraculously I did, but I was very nervous about that and of course I wanted to be good and didn't want to let everyone down."

It is amazing that Madonna still gets nervous, considering she has performed alongside the likes of Tom Hanks, Warren Beatty, Sean Penn, Geena

Davis, Antonio Banderas and Al Pacino to name but a few. She has even been a Bond girl of sorts, with a cameo in 2002's *Die Another Day*, a film for which she also provided the title track.

And speaking of Beatty and Penn, Madonna's love life has had the press in a spin since she first burst on to the music scene. It's the one area of her life where she has not always been able to retain control. The road to contentment has not always been easy, but she does seem to have found true and lasting happiness with her second husband British director Guy Ritchie.

Although critics have accused her of only living for the press attention, Madonna has managed to maintain a private life, although she has to struggle harder than most to keep it private. Recently she forced a public enquiry into a new right-to-roam law that will allow ramblers near her Georgian mansion home in Wiltshire. Also, she had to remove the 12-feet high security gates that had been installed, because she had failed to apply for necessary planning permission.

Madonna has been let down by people she has trusted in the past but she is now surrounded by a tight group of friends she can depend on. The fact that no one sold the story about what happened at

MADONNA

MEGASTAR

Madonna and Ritchie's wedding proves how loyal friends and family are to the superstar.

And there can be no doubt that the arrivals of Lourdes in 1996 and Rocco in 2000 has changed everyone's favourite shock queen. Although claims she has calmed down can always be countered with another headline-grabbing stunt, Madonna has certainly been a model mum to her two children. And while she doesn't hide her children away from the world's media, she does encourage them to live as normal a life as possible, with some strict house rules. For example, not only does the superstar admit to carefully monitoring what television her children are allowed to watch, but she has also banned newspapers and magazines from her house, telling Larry King on his chat show, Larry King Live: "They are full of lies – I don't want to have anything to do with them. It's just a rule in our house – nobody can bring in newspapers or magazines."

Her new tour, 2004's Reinvention, promises to contain all the classic hits, although according to press rumours, some of them are to be reworked or 'reinvented' and brought up to date. Within days of announcing the dates, most of the shows were sold out, with demand for tickets as high as ever,

MADONNA

breaking many sales' records.

Madonna has become the living legend who drinks at the local pub. The living embodiment of the American dream who chooses to live in England. Madonna will never be easy to define, and her fans would certainly never want her to be. What is unique about Madonna is her ability to constantly evolve without losing the star quality that is so rare, but that she possesses in abundance. She is truly one of a kind.

13

Discography

MADONNA

ALBUMS

1983 Madonna
1984 Like a Virgin
1986 True Blue
1987 Who's That Girl
1987 You Can Dance
1989 Like a Prayer
1990 I'm Breathless
1990 The Immaculate Collection
1992 Erotica
1994 Bedtime Stories
1995 Something to Remember
1996 Evita
1998 Ray of Light
2000 The Next Best Thing
2000 Music
2001 GHV2
2002 Die Another Day
2003 American Life

14

Filmography

MOVIES

Crazy For You (1985)
Singer at Club
A Certain Sacrifice (1985)
Bruna
Desperately Seeking Susan (1985)
Susan
Shanghai Surprise (1986)
Gloria Tatlock
Who's That Girl? (1987)
Nikki Finn
Bloodhounds of Broadway (1989)
Hortense Hathaway
Dick Tracy (1990)
Breathless Mahoney
In Bed With Madonna (1991)
Herself
Shadows and Fog (1992)
Marie
A League of Their Own (1992)
'All-The-Way-Mae' Mordabito
Dangerous Game (1993)
Sarah Jennings
Body of Evidence (1993)
Rebecca Carlson

MADONNA

FILMOGRAPHY

Blue in the Face (1995)
Singing Telegram
Four Rooms (1995)
Elspeth
Girl 6 (1996)
Boss number 3
Evita (1996)
Eva 'Evita' Duarte de Perón
The Next Best Thing (2000)
Abbie Reynolds
The Hire: Star (2001)
Star
Swept Away (2002)
Amber Leighton
Die Another Day (2002)
Verity

BIOGRAPHIES

OTHER BOOKS IN THE SERIES

Also available in the series:

OTHER BOOKS IN THE SERIES

JENNIFER ANISTON

She's been a Friend to countless millions worldwide, and overcame numerous hurdles to rise to the very top of her field. From a shy girl with a dream of being a famous actress, through being reduced to painting scenery for high school plays, appearing in a series of flop TV shows and one rather bad movie, Jennifer Aniston has persevered, finally finding success at the very top of the TV tree.

Bringing the same determination that got her a part on the world's best-loved TV series to her attempts at a film career, she's also worked her way from rom-com cutie up to serious, respected actress and box office draw, intelligently combining indie, cult and comedy movies into a blossoming career which looks set to shoot her to the heights of Hollywood's A-list. She's also found love with one of the world's most desirable men. Is Jennifer Aniston the ultimate Hollywood Renaissance woman? It would seem she's got more than a shot at such a title, as indeed, she seems to have it all, even if things weren't always that way. Learn all about Aniston's rise to fame in this compelling biography.

OTHER BOOKS IN THE SERIES

DAVID BECKHAM

This book covers the amazing life of the boy from East London who has not only become a world class footballer and the captain of England, but also an idol to millions, and probably the most famous man in Britain.

His biography tracks his journey, from the playing fields of Chingford to the Bernabau. It examines how he joined his beloved Manchester United and became part of a golden generation of talent that led to United winning trophies galore.

Beckham's parallel personal life is also examined, as he moved from tongue-tied football-obsessed kid to suitor of a Spice Girl, to one half of Posh & Becks, the most famous celebrity couple in Britain – perhaps the world. His non-footballing activities, his personal indulgences and changing styles have invited criticism, and even abuse, but his football talent has confounded the critics, again and again.

The biography looks at his rise to fame and his relationship with Posh, as well as his decision to leave Manchester for Madrid. Has it affected his relationship with Posh? What will the latest controversy over his sex life mean for celebrity's royal couple? And will he come back to play in England again?

OTHER BOOKS IN THE SERIES

GEORGE CLOONEY

The tale of George Clooney's astonishing career is an epic every bit as riveting as one of his blockbuster movies. It's a story of tenacity and determination, of fame and infamy, a story of succeeding on your own terms regardless of the risks. It's also a story of emergency rooms, batsuits, tidal waves and killer tomatoes, but let's not get ahead of ourselves.

Born into a family that, by Sixties' Kentucky standards, was dripping with show business glamour, George grew up seeing the hard work and heartache that accompanied a life in the media spotlight.

By the time stardom came knocking for George Clooney, it found a level-headed and mature actor ready and willing to embrace the limelight, while still indulging a lifelong love of partying and practical jokes. A staunchly loyal friend and son, a bachelor with a taste for the high life, a vocal activist for the things he believes and a born and bred gentleman; through failed sitcoms and blockbuster disasters, through artistic credibility and box office success, George Clooney has remained all of these things...and much, much more. Prepare to meet Hollywood's most fascinating megastar in this riveting biography.

OTHER BOOKS IN THE SERIES

BILLY CONNOLLY

In a 2003 London Comedy Poll to find Britain's favourite comedian, Billy Connolly came out on top. It's more than just Billy Connolly's all-round comic genius that puts him head and shoulders above the rest. Connolly has also proved himself to be an accomplished actor with dozens of small and big screen roles to his name. In 2003, he could be seen in *The Last Samurai* with Tom Cruise.

Connolly has also cut the mustard in the USA, 'breaking' that market in a way that chart-topping pop groups since The Beatles and the Stones have invariably failed to do, let alone mere stand-up comedians. Of course, like The Beatles and the Stones, Billy Connolly has been to the top of the pop charts too with D.I.V.O.R.C.E. in 1975.

On the way he's experienced heartache of his own with a difficult childhood and a divorce of his own, found the time and energy to bring up five children, been hounded by the press on more than one occasion, and faced up to some considerable inner demons. But Billy Connolly is a survivor. Now in his 60s, he's been in show business for all of 40 years, and 2004 finds him still touring. This exciting biography tells the story an extraordinary entertainer.

OTHER BOOKS IN THE SERIES

ROBERT DE NIRO

Robert De Niro is cinema's greatest chameleon. Snarling one minute, smirking the next, he's straddled Hollywood for a quarter of a century, making his name as a serious character actor, in roles ranging from psychotic taxi drivers to hardened mobsters. The scowls and pent-up violence may have won De Niro early acclaim but, ingeniously, he's now playing them for laughs, poking fun at the tough guy image he so carefully cultivated. Ever the perfectionist, De Niro holds nothing back on screen, but in real life he is a very private man – he thinks of himself as just another guy doing a job. Some job, some guy. There's more to the man than just movies. De Niro helped New York pick itself up after the September 11 terrorist attacks on the Twin Towers by launching the TriBeCa Film Festival and inviting everyone downtown. He runs several top-class restaurants and has dated some of the most beautiful women in the world, least of all supermodel Naomi Campbell. Now in his 60s, showered with awards and a living legend, De Niro's still got his foot on the pedal. There are six, yes six, films coming your way in 2004. In this latest biography, you'll discover all about his latest roles and the life of this extraordinary man.

OTHER BOOKS IN THE SERIES

MICHAEL DOUGLAS

Douglas may have been a shaggy-haired member of a hippy commune in the Sixties but just like all the best laidback, free-loving beatniks, he's gone on to blaze a formidable career, in both acting and producing.

In a career that has spanned nearly 40 years so far, Douglas has produced a multitude of hit movies including the classic *One Flew Over The Cuckoo's Nest* and *The China Syndrome* through to box office smashes such as *Starman* and *Face/Off*.

His acting career has been equally successful – from *Romancing The Stone* to *Wall Street* to *Fatal Attraction*, Douglas's roles have shown that he isn't afraid of putting himself on the line when up there on the big screen.

His relationship with his father; his stay in a top clinic to combat his drinking problem; the breakdown of his first marriage; and his publicised clash with the British media have all compounded to create the image of a man who's transformed himself from being the son of Hollywood legend Kirk Douglas, into Kirk Douglas being the dad of Hollywood legend, Michael Douglas.

HUGH GRANT

He's the Oxford fellow who stumbled into acting, the middle-class son of a carpet salesman who became famous for bumbling around stately homes and posh weddings. The megastar actor who claims he doesn't like acting, but has appeared in over 40 movies and TV shows.

On screen he's romanced a glittering array of Hollywood's hottest actresses, and tackled medical conspiracies and the mafia. Off screen he's hogged the headlines with his high profile girlfriend as well as finding lifelong notoriety after a little Divine intervention in Los Angeles.

Hugh Grant is Britain's biggest movie star, an actor whose talent for comedy has often been misjudged by those who assume he simply plays himself.

From bit parts in Nottingham theatre, through comedy revues at the Edinburgh Fringe, and on to the top of the box office charts, Hugh has remained constant – charming, witty and ever so slightly sarcastic, obsessed with perfection and performance while winking to his audience as if to say: "This is all awfully silly, isn't it?" Don't miss this riveting biography.

OTHER BOOKS IN THE SERIES

MICHAEL JACKSON

Friday 29 August 1958 was not a special day in Gary, Indiana, and indeed Gary, was far from being a special place. But it was on this day and in this location that the world's greatest entertainer was to be born, Michael Joseph Jackson.

The impact that this boy was destined to have on the world of entertainment could never have been estimated. Here we celebrate Michael Jackson's extraordinary talents, and plot the defining events over his forty-year career. This biography explores the man behind the myth, and gives an understanding of what drives this special entertainer.

In 1993, there was an event that was to rock Jackson's world. His friendship with a twelve-year-old boy and the subsequent allegations resulted in a lawsuit, a fall in record sales and a long road to recovery. Two marriages, three children and 10 years later there is a feeling of déja vu as Jackson again deals with more controversy. Without doubt, 2004 proves to be the most important year in the singer's life. Whatever that future holds for Jackson, his past is secured, there has never been and there will never again be anything quite like Michael Jackson.

OTHER BOOKS IN THE SERIES

NICOLE KIDMAN

On 23 March 2003 Nicole Kidman won the Oscar for Best Actress for her role as Virginia Woolf in *The Hours*. That was the night that marked Nicole Kidman's acceptance into the upper echelons of Hollywood royalty. She had certainly come a long way from the 'girlfriend' roles she played when she first arrived in Hollywood – in films such as *Billy Bathgate* and *Batman Forever* – although even then she managed to inject her 'pretty girl' roles with an edge that made her acting stand out. And she was never merely content to be Mrs Cruise, movie star's wife. Although she stood dutifully behind her then husband in 1993 when he was given his star on the Hollywood Walk of Fame, Nicole got a star of her own 10 years later, in 2003.

Not only does Nicole Kidman have stunning good looks and great pulling power at the box office, she also has artistic credibility. But Nicole has earned the respect of her colleagues, working hard and turning in moving performances from a very early age. Although she dropped out of school at 16, no one doubts the intelligence and passion that are behind the fiery redhead's acting career, which includes television and stage work, as well as films. Find out how Kidman became one of Hollywood's most respected actresses in this compelling biography.

OTHER BOOKS IN THE SERIES

JENNIFER LOPEZ

There was no suggestion that the Jennifer Lopez of the early Nineties would become the accomplished actress, singer and icon that she is today. Back then she was a dancer on the popular comedy show *In Living Color* – one of the Fly Girls, the accompaniment, not the main event. In the early days she truly was Jenny from the block; the Bronx native of Puerto Rican descent – another hopeful from the east coast pursuing her dreams in the west.

Today, with two marriages under her belt, three multi-platinum selling albums behind her and an Oscar-winning hunk as one of her ex-boyfriends, she is one of the most talked about celebrities of the day. Jennifer Lopez is one of the most celebrated Hispanic actresses of all time.

Her beauty, body and famous behind, are lusted after by men and envied by women throughout the world. She has proven that she can sing, dance and act. Yet her critics dismiss her as a diva without talent. And the criticisms are not just about her work, some of them are personal. But what is the reality? Who is Jennifer Lopez, where did she come from and how did get to where she is now? This biography aims to separate fact from fiction to reveal the real Jennifer Lopez.

OTHER BOOKS IN THE SERIES

BRAD PITT

From the launch pad that was his scene stealing turn in Thelma And Louise as the sexual-enlightening bad boy. To his character-driven performances in dramas such as *Legends of the Fall* through to his Oscar-nominated work in *Twelve Monkeys* and the dark and razor-edged Tyler Durden in *Fight Club*, Pitt has never rested on his laurels. Or his good looks.

And the fact that his love life has garnered headlines all over the world hasn't hindered Brad Pitt's profile away from the screen either – linked by the press to many women, his relationships with the likes of Juliette Lewis and Gwyneth Paltrow. Then of course, in 2000, we had the Hollywood fairytale ending when he tied the silk knot with Jennifer Aniston.

Pitt's impressive track record as a superstar, sex symbol and credible actor looks set to continue as he has three films lined up for release over the next year – as Achilles in the Wolfgang Peterson-helmed Troy; Rusty Ryan in the sequel *Ocean's Twelve* and the titular Mr Smith in the thriller *Mr & Mrs Smith* alongside Angelina Jolie. Pitt's ever-growing success shows no signs of abating. Discover all about Pitt's meteoric rise from rags to riches in this riveting biography.

OTHER BOOKS IN THE SERIES

SHANE RICHIE

Few would begrudge the current success of 40-year-old Shane Richie. To get where he is today, Shane has had a rather bumpy roller coaster ride that has seen the hard working son of poor Irish immigrants endure more than his fair share of highs and lows – financially, professionally and personally.

In the space of four decades he has amused audiences at school plays, realised his childhood dream of becoming a Pontins holiday camp entertainer, experienced homelessness, beat his battle with drink, became a millionaire then lost the lot. He's worked hard and played hard.

When the producers of *EastEnders* auditioned Shane for a role in the top TV soap, they decided not to give him the part, but to create a new character especially for him. That character was Alfie Moon, manager of the Queen Vic pub, and very quickly Shane's TV alter ego has become one of the most popular soap characters in Britain. This biography is the story of a boy who had big dreams and never gave up on turning those dreams into reality.

OTHER BOOKS IN THE SERIES

JONNY WILKINSON

"There's 35 seconds to go, this is the one. It's coming back for Jonny Wilkinson. He drops for World Cup glory. It's over! He's done it! Jonny Wilkinson is England's Hero yet again..."

That memorable winning drop kick united the nation, and lead to the start of unprecedented victory celebrations throughout the land. In the split seconds it took for the ball to leave his boot and slip through the posts, Wilkinson's life was to change forever. It wasn't until three days later, when the squad flew back to Heathrow and were met with a rapturous reception, that the enormity of their win, began to sink in.

Like most overnight success stories, Wilkinson's journey has been a long and dedicated one. He spent 16 years 'in rehearsal' before achieving his finest performance, in front of a global audience of 22 million, on that rainy evening in Telstra Stadium, Sydney.

But how did this modest self-effacing 24-year-old become England's new number one son? This biography follows Jonny's journey to international stardom. Find out how he caught the rugby bug, what and who his earliest influences were and what the future holds for our latest English sporting hero.

OTHER BOOKS IN THE SERIES

ROBBIE WILLIAMS

Professionally, things can't get much better for Robbie Williams. In 2002 he signed the largest record deal in UK history when he re-signed with EMI. The following year he performed to over 1.5 million fans on his European tour, breaking all attendance records at Knebworth with three consecutive sell-out gigs.

Since going solo Robbie Williams has achieved five number one hit singles, five number one hit albums; 10 Brits and three Ivor Novello awards. When he left the highly successful boy band Take That in 1995 his future seemed far from rosy. He got off to a shaky start. His nemesis, Gary Barlow, had already recorded two number one singles and the press had virtually written Williams off. But then in December 1997, he released his Christmas single, *Angels.*

Angels re-launched his career – it remained in the Top 10 for 11 weeks. Since then Robbie has gone from strength to strength, both as a singer and a natural showman. His live videos are a testament to his performing talent and his promotional videos are works of art.

This biography tells of Williams' journey to the top – stopping off on the way to take a look at his songs, his videos, his shows, his relationships, his rows, his record deals and his demons.